THE DATA WELFARE STATE

Anne Kaun
Anu Masso

THE DATA WELFARE STATE

Sage

1 Oliver's Yard
55 City Road
London EC1Y 1SP

2455 Teller Road
Thousand Oaks
California 91320

Unit No 323-333, Third Floor, F-Block
International Trade Tower,
Nehru Place, New Delhi 110 019

8 Marina View Suite 43-053
Asia Square Tower 1
Singapore 018960

Editor: Michael Ainsley
Editorial assistant: Pippa Wills
Production editor: Nicola Marshall
Marketing manager: Fauzia Eastwood
Cover design: Victoria Bridal
Typeset by: TNQ Tech Pvt. Ltd.
Indexer: TNQ Tech Pvt. Ltd.

© Anne Kaun and Anu Masso 2025

Published in collaboration with the Data Justice Lab as part of the Data Justice Series.

Apart from any fair dealing for the purposes of research, private study, or criticism or review, as permitted under the Copyright, Designs and Patents Act, 1988, this publication may not be reproduced, stored or transmitted in any form, or by any means, without the prior permission in writing of the publisher, or in the case of reprographic reproduction, in accordance with the terms of licences issued by the Copyright Licensing Agency. Enquiries concerning reproduction outside those terms should be sent to the publisher.

Library of Congress Control Number: 2024942321

British Library Cataloguing in Publication data

A catalogue record for this book is available from the British Library

ISBN 978-1-5296-6780-6
ISBN 978-1-5296-6779-0 (pbk)

Contents

Preface   vii

About the Authors   xi

Introduction   1

1 Evolving Data Welfare State   15

2 The Mundanisation of Algorithmic Public Services   43

3 Experiences of Data Welfare   65

4 (Re-)Configuring Data Welfare   87

Conclusion: Crisis in the Welfare Question: Rethinking the Welfare State in the Age of Automation   105

Index   113

Preface

In recent years, the promise of automation within welfare institutions has gained traction as a solution to address budget constraints and shifting demographics. The deployment of algorithmic systems is often heralded as a means to reduce costs and enhance fairness in decision-making processes. However, the notion of efficiency has come under increasing scrutiny. Critics have highlighted the substantial costs associated with automation projects, including software development and the training of case workers to navigate evolving software infrastructures.

This book delves into the complexities and contradictions that arise within welfare automation initiatives, as well as the profound challenges they pose to core public values. We explore the day-to-day practices of case workers as they grapple with automation, delve into the experiences of citizens affected by these changes and examine the broader implications for the social and political fabric of welfare provision. Our focus is on the inherent contradictions that fuel the uncertainty of technological transformation within the context of shifting political landscapes. As we will demonstrate, technology rarely unfolds as smoothly as envisioned. At the same time, we are decentering technology itself and instead highlight the people in and around datafication infrastructures.

There is a pressing need for an in-depth exploration of the intersection between automation and the transformation of welfare states. We engage with the implications of sorting, matching and predictive algorithms within the realm of welfare provision. Our research agenda draws inspiration from datafication research while focusing on the realm of welfare. Hence, the title of the book. The data welfare state also serves as a theoretical framework here. The focus on welfare shifts the spotlight from the private sector to the automation of public administration and welfare provision. We use 'data welfare' as a heuristic tool to assess the consequences of the growing delegation of cultural practices – such as categorisation, classification, sorting and hierarchisation – into digital systems like algorithms and artificial intelligence. This phenomenon – raising 'algorithmic culture' – underpins our exploration of how automation shapes and reshapes the welfare state.

This book tackles the social and political implications of digitalisation and datafication and, more specifically, automation. We draw upon original empirical research to illuminate the inherent contradictions within automation projects and the evolving concept of welfare in the context of digital technologies. These insights are gleaned from case studies spanning the Estonian and Swedish welfare state models with some excursions into the German system. The book aims to contribute to answering the question how to harness data-based automation in a manner that aligns with the core principles of the welfare state. We offer insights for charting a path forward that balances technological advancements with the preservation of fundamental welfare state values.

This book is intended for a diverse readership, encompassing researchers interested in critical data studies, digital transformations in public administration and those exploring the social and political implications of big data, smart technology and artificial intelligence. It will be of particular interest to undergraduate and graduate students pursuing degrees in public administration, sociology, media and communication studies, as well as media technologies and design. However, its broad relevance extends to anyone seeking a deeper understanding of these pressing issues in the digital age.

This book is poised to engage readers on a global scale. Through an exploration of distinct welfare regimes, it sheds light on the contextual nuances that underpin the automation of welfare, providing a rich historical and political backdrop. While welfare contexts of Germany, Estonia and Sweden serve as prime examples of corporatist, social democratic and post-communist welfare regimes, the book's findings transcend national boundaries. Its insights resonate with diverse welfare contexts worldwide, and therefore we hope, making it a valuable resource for a broad international readership seeking to understand the implications of welfare automation.

The book's scope is rooted in a broader historical context of social transformations within welfare states and the evolving concept of the common good. While specific technologies and technological solutions may evolve over time, the discussions within these pages are firmly situated within a historical trajectory of technological change and its far-reaching social and political consequences. This approach ensures that the book's insights remain pertinent, both within contemporary discourse and as part of a larger historical narrative. This book delves into the realm of datafication of public services and welfare institutions, illuminating the contours of the emerging data welfare state. It begins with a critical premise: the pervasive digitalisation, a prerequisite for datafication and data-based automation, has wrought fundamental changes in the welfare state. These transformations bear significant consequences for citizens, affecting not only the direct outcomes of welfare provision but also reshaping the dynamics of state-citizen relations. The book places particular emphasis on the implications of algorithmic automation for trust and public values, as perceived by the individuals caught within this process. This encompasses case workers operating across various public agencies, navigating the intricacies of automation infrastructures, and citizens whose data underpin these automation projects.

Rather than viewing automation as a mere administrative task, this book firmly links technological questions to broader political issues. While the industry often portrays the implementation of new technological solutions as seamless, empirical case studies have consistently revealed a starkly different reality. Not all citizens experience digitalisation, datafication and automation in the same way. The process is fraught with conflicts, contradictions and inherent biases, which can lead to injustices even as it promises enhanced services for select individuals. These contradictions and their ramifications for citizens stand at the core of this book's explorations, offering a critical examination of the intersection between technology and politics within the context of welfare automation.

We believe that a comprehensive book on the intersection of automated decision-making and welfare state transformation is urgently required to delve into the ramifications of sorting, matching and predictive algorithms in welfare provision for citizens.

The work on this book was generously funded by the Foundation for Baltic and East European Studies (grant agreement number: S2-20-0007). Parts of the analytical work have been conducted with collaborators and have been published in different versions as:

- Anu Masso, Tayfun Kasapoglu, Vasilis Galis & Anne Kaun (2024) Citizens' Perspectives on Platformisation of Police Work: A Scenario and Story-Based Exploration in Estonia and Sweden. Information, *Communication & Society*, https://doi.org/10.1080/1369118X.2024.2333842
- Anu Masso, Anne Kaun & Colin van Noordt (2023) Basic values in artificial intelligence: comparative factor analysis in Estonia, Germany, and Sweden. *AI & Society*. https://doi.org/10.1007/s00146-023-01750-w
- Anne Kaun, Anders O. Larsson, Anu Masso (2023) Automating Public Administration: Citizens' Attitudes Towards Automated Decision-Making Across Estonia, Sweden, and Germany. *Information, Communication & Society*, https://doi.org/10.1080/1369118X.2023.2205493

Anne Kaun would like to thank the department for media and communication studies at Södertörn University for support and an inspiring environment. In particular, she would like to thank the Digital Welfare Research team that includes Agnes Liminga, Maris Männiste and Amela Muratspahić. Furthermore, Anne would like to thank Anders O. Larsson for the collaboration and analytical skills.

Anu Masso would like to express her gratitude to the Ragnar Nurkse Department of Innovation and Governance at Tallinn University of Technology (TalTech) for hosting the AUTO-WELF project, and to the Data Lab team for the inspiring discussions. Additionally, Anu is grateful to Tayfun Kasaspoglu for the collaboration and his qualitative analytical skills, and Colin van Noordt, Vasilis Galis, and Anders O. Larsson for co-authoring the articles that form the foundation of this book.

The work was produced without the help of generative artificial intelligence; however, parts of the transcriptions of interview material, some parts of the illustrative vignettes, and language check were supported by artificial intelligence. After using the AI tool, the authors reviewed and edited the text as needed and take full responsibility for the content of the publication. The two authors have equally contributed to the writing of the book. Anu Masso has mainly been responsible for the quantitative analyses, whereas Anne Kaun has had the oversight over the qualitative analyses. The order of authors mentioning is merely alphabetical and does not reflect the workload or share of responsibility.

About the Authors

Anne Kaun is a Professor of Media and Communication Studies at Södertörn University, Stockholm Sweden and a Wallenberg Academy Fellow. The past years she has been studying the democratic implications of automated decision-making, artificial intelligence, and digitalization in the welfare sector. Previously, she has engaged with projects concerning prisons and media infrastructures, media trust during the pandemic as well as digital activism and memory culture.

Anu Masso is an Associate Professor of Big Data in Social Sciences at the Ragnar Nurkse Department of Innovation and Governance, Tallinn University of Technology. Her research focuses on the social dimensions of data, algorithms, and AI, as well as social transformations and spatial mobilities. She is also known for her work on social science methods and methodologies and serves as an expert on the societal implications of data-based technologies.

Introduction

Scene 1 at the public library: A man has been sitting for at least 30 minutes in front of one of the workstations and he is getting increasingly nervous and impatient, in a desperate rather than angry manner. At some point he decides he needs help and turns to the librarian working in the info desk. "I need help, I need to submit a form to the Insurance agency, and I just cannot make it work. Can you please, please help me?". The librarian hesitates a second, exhales and follows him to the computer with the note "I guess it's a problem with your bank-ID, its usually the bank-ID that is causing problems".

Scene 2 at the welfare service center: a woman is sitting in the waiting area for her number to be called. After 10 minutes a service worker wearing a green shirt with white letters saying *e-days do yourself an e-favor* enters the area checking a smart phone and calling the next number in line. The woman who waited patiently approaches her. They walk over to a computer station at a high desk together and the service worker asks what she needs help with. The woman explains that she has received an email about her child benefits. She is asked to submit additional information from her employer and about her salary. She is directed to the application or website of the insurance agency, but just cannot find her way. She needs help. The case worker unlocks the screen of the stationary computer and navigates the woman through the platform, while never touching the keyboard or mouse herself. The woman is supposed to learn by doing the clicking herself. Help to digital self-help is the slogan of the welfare service centers.

Scene 3 at the jail: A man in his forties has been waiting for his trial for 8 months. He has been placed in solitary confinement by the prosecutor, which means he will only meet his lawyer and potentially volunteers from the RedCross. No family members or friends are allowed to visit, and he has one designated incarcerated person that he gets to hang out with for in total 3 hours per day. He has been sleeping badly from the first night and this pattern has not improved ever since. He finally has called for help from the staff describing his problem. One day later they bring a Fitbit to his room. "You will wear this device for the next week and we will know whether you need help with your sleep". When the results come in the man is surprised, according to the wearable he has been sleeping exceptionally well. He feels the exhaustion of the past months running through his body.

These are stories that we have encountered in this or similar ways in the past years during our fieldwork in marginal spaces of the welfare state: at public libraries, welfare service centres and prisons. The problems that emerge in the stories are expressions of frictions in data welfare, scenes in which human collaboration is crucial: being lost in public agency applications, trying to do the right thing on platforms that are hard to navigate and digital devices telling different stories than our own embodied experiences. They seem both mundane and special, outside of what many of us have experienced ourselves in connection with digital welfare, but – and that is our main argument – turning to the margins and the data frictions that emerge there will help us improve digital services not only for the marginalised and vulnerable groups but also for all. Minna Ruckenstein (2023) highlights that the notion of friction is also used by engineers and designers. It is mainly used to depict something to be diminished as much as possible in the design process. Engineers and designers primarily seek to develop perfect human–machine loops. The main goal is frictionless living enabled by computational tools, a perfectly smooth symbiosis of man and machine. For Tsing and Ruckenstein, friction is not only standing merely in the way of a tech dream but also a societally attuned notion that is connected with resilience. Tsing and Ruckenstein argue further that friction makes connections influential and effective and 'gets in the way of the smooth operation of global power'. Frictions highlight and make visible inequalities and unveil the well-oiled machine as impossible (Ruckenstein, 2023, p. 8).

The stories above illustrate that the smooth, frictionless interaction with the digital welfare machine is rarely the case. Even with new methods of designing digital and data-based tools, frictions remain and will remain. So, what do we do with that then? Is the solution to develop better platforms? To improve data skills among citizens? Will there ever be a smooth data welfare state? The marginal places we have visited for our research have made clear that digital frictions make inequalities, power relations and also mundane ways of relating to complex technological systems visible. Instead of striving for the perfect data welfare machine, we need to embrace and sit with the inconvenience, the ambivalence and the digital frictions. As Minna Ruckenstein (2023) argues:

> the ambivalence that accompanies reactions to corporate uses of personal data calls for approaches that do not try to smooth tensions away but can comfortably address the contradictions and balancing acts involved. (p. 8)

In that sense, even with data tools, life is never a smooth ride and we need to address the emerging tensions. Instead of aiming for the perfectly smooth welfare machine, we collectively need to imagine a system of welfare that provides for all according to their needs and capabilities. Data tools might be part of the processes of finding out how and in what ways this can be done, but they should not be the starting point. This book aims at contributing to this process by exploring the current state of data welfare and the history of how we got there.

Data-Based Automation and Welfare

Today, the discussion on cognitive, data-based automation, that is, the delegation of work that is not mechanical but contains solutions to complex problems, is dominant. Some predict, for example, that new areas such as communication services will be automated and thus many jobs will disappear (for a critical reading of books that in different variations claim this, see Judy Wajcman (2017)). In connection with this development, it has been discussed that the state must support those who lose their jobs due to automation. One way to respond to large-scale automation is the citizen's wage or universal basic income, which means a basic income for everyone regardless of whether they work or not.

However, Aaron Benanva (2020) questions whether an universal basic income would lead to more welfare for all and economic equality. He argues that universal basic income rather maintains the prevailing order and distribution of resources in society. He is also critical of the view that it is automation in general that leads to large-scale unemployment. He argues that it is other processes such as financialisation that have led to the structural unemployment we see today. In contrast to Benanva, Aaron Bastani (2019) argues that automation with the help of artificial intelligence (AI) and algorithms enables a new social order under communist auspices where people are freed from repetitive and meaningless labour.

What Is Automation and Datafication?

The history of automation can be divided into three eras: industrialisation associated with factory work and the deskilling of labour (until 1900), knowledge-based technological change (1900–1970) and labour polarisation (since the 1970s). Some of the major changes during the industrial revolution are associated with technological development, such as the steam engine and large mechanical looms. Automation here was about the emergence of factory work and how factory work was made more efficient. During the early stage of industrialisation – dominated by factory work and deskilling – the lives of many in England deteriorated, Frey (2019) argues. He further suggests that automation in factories allowed women and children to enter the workforce being less paid while higher paid workers remained unemployed. This also affected public health. Frey writes:

> (...) William Alison, a distinguished professor of medicine at Edinburgh University, insisted that low wages were a cause of poor public health. Unemployment, disappearing incomes, and poor nutrition, he argued were critical factors in explaining health conditions of ordinary people. (Frey, 2019, p. 115)

Social welfare thus deteriorated during the early industrial revolution. It would take several decades and active organisation of the labour movement before the situation changed with the emergence of the welfare state in post-war Europe. During the second phase of automation up to the 1970s, the level of education also improved and there is thus talk of a reskilling of the workforce, with new, for example, computer-based, occupations requiring new skills and training.

Automation today builds on large-scale datafication, namely turning increasing aspects of peoples' lives and practices as well as societal institutions into data points (van Dijck, 2014) that is underpinned by the ideology of dataism. Dataism proposes that digital data provide a clear form of objectivity and a new way of knowing the world and hence acting on it. This ideology underpins many automation projects in the public sector today.

What Is Welfare?

Welfare refers to people's living conditions and is often associated with 'the good life' or, as sociologist Erik Allardt (1975) writes, 'people need a decent material standard of living (to have), contacts with their fellow human beings (to love) and opportunities both to actively influence society and to be treated as a person, not just as a thing (to be)' (p. 27). However, welfare and the good society is notoriously difficult to define. Is it about the perception of living standard? Is it about objective economic and social position? Or a combination of both? How does welfare relate to needs, capabilities and values? These are questions that have been tackled by welfare research for many decades but are still hard to answer. According to Raymond Williams (1976), welfare is a keyword of modern society. It was initially used to indicate happiness or prosperity. Employing the term to depict organised welfare through institutionalised provision for basic needs emerged first in the 20th century and the idea of the welfare state was only mentioned during the Second World War. The notion of the welfare state is built on normative ideas of universalism, equality and decommodification (Jakobsson et al., 2023). Based on these principles, the welfare state relates to measures to enhance social cohesion, as well as a balancing of risks within society while preserving human dignity (Jakobsson et al., 2023). One fundamental principle of welfare is the idea of providing for basic needs to all, but a more ambitious outlook considers different capabilities of people and promotes measures for human flourishing accordingly.

But what does state-organised welfare mean? According to Lindert (2004), one can distinguish between different stages of progressivity of welfare measures. The most basic step is basic support and unemployment compensation, pensions and public health care and public basic education. Second more progressive measures are housing allowances and further education and the third most progressive step is state-funded higher education.

Gösta Esping-Andersen associates ideas about the welfare state with T. H. Marshall's concept of social citizenship, namely guaranteed social rights. Esping-Andersen (1990) argues that this means first and foremost the decommodification of the individual from the market. He further argues that the status of citizen in a welfare state will replace their class position and that the welfare state brings together the market, the family and the state. Esping-Andersen argues that different ways of organising welfare have resulted in different welfare regimes, where he distinguishes between the liberal regime with a focus on individual responsibility (e.g. the United States, Canada and the United Kingdom), the social democratic welfare regime with a focus on universality and equal access to welfare that characterises the Nordic countries and the conservative welfare regime characterised by a strong position of the family and labour market actors, for example, Germany, France and Italy.

Esping-Andersen derives the idea of decommodification from Karl Polanyi, who discusses reembedding, namely the regulation of markets. Polanyi (1944) suggests that there are certain fictitious goods such as land, money and labour that are not naturally produced for sale on a market. Instead, they are actually framed in social contexts and not conceived as products but during the rise of capitalism are commodified.

What they have in common, however, is that the welfare state is supposed to respond to challenges for its citizens that arise due to the market or needs that the market fails to meet (market failure) through public spending financed by taxes, for example.

The question then arises as to why the idea of the welfare state arises at all. Social policies such as social insurance and the like arose to even out conflicts in societies. Bismarck's earlier reforms, for example, were designed to address social conflicts in the German Empire at the end of the 19th century. These included health insurance, accident insurance, old age and disability insurance. Thus, it was primarily the organisation of the working class and their protests against poor living and working conditions that had to be addressed, rather than a benevolent state wanting to support the population. According to Lindert (2004), it is the active organisation of the working class that led to the emergence of the welfare state and public spending to support the population. However, Lindert's main argument is that public spending on welfare measures that promote, for example, health, prevent large-scale poverty and promote education leads to greater economic growth and does not, as many have previously argued, limit development or growth.

The Datafied Welfare State and Automated Decision-Making

Jon Agar (2003) has traced the mechanisation and later computerisation of the British state that was accompanied with ideas about the general-purpose government machine that include mechanical, digital as well as human components. While it has been pointed out that the welfare state has always already been datafied collecting information about citizens in a systematic manner and on large scale, the digitalisation has accelerated this tendency (Dencik & Kaun, 2020). New areas, practices and characteristics are being datafied and made trackable and traceable. The main focus of this book is on the frictions in transformative processes related to introducing, experimenting with and using the automated decision-making solutions in the welfare domains.

Our starting point is that the introduction of data-based technologies in public administration has led to the emergence of a data welfare state that takes different shapes depending on the specific political context as well as historical preconditions. However, data welfare states share a strong push towards algorithmic automation, which has among others consequences for how citizens are both constructed as well as how they relate to state institutions (Fourcade, 2021). Often the introduction of algorithmic systems (van Toorn & Scully, 2023) is supposed to compensate for considerable cuts in resources for specific welfare domains as Redden et al. (2020) have shown for automation projects within child welfare projects. Projects to foster the data welfare state are framed in terms of efficiency and effectiveness as well as increased fairness and justice as human error is diminished. Emerging projects have been explored within different welfare domains including social services (e.g von Toorn & Scully, 2023), education (Sophus Lai et al., 2023) and health (Högberg et al., 2023).

The data welfare state emerges in different expressions including front end digitalisation such as digital platforms for accessing and interacting with public agencies to backend digitalisation such as automated application processing. One prominent feature that has gained increasing interest and has direct implications for citizens is automated decision-making (Högberg, 2023). Automated decision-making refers to the process of implementing and delegating tasks to digital systems – both rule- and knowledge-based. One precondition for automated decision-making is the process of datafication, namely the quantification of social life at large and the production of big data (Mayer-Schönberger & Cukier, 2013). These changes are already underway in areas such as education, labour and warfare, through – for example – new forms of algorithmic governance (Eubanks, 2018; Kennedy, 2016; Mosco, 2017; O'Neil, 2016). Algorithmic automated decision-making or decision support systems are procedures that utilise automatically executed decision-making algorithms to perform an action (Spielkamp, 2019). With the help of mathematical models, big data or the combination of different registers, algorithms issue a decision – for example – on an application for social benefits. While it has been argued that civil servants are freed from repetitive and monotonous tasks with the help of algorithms (Engin & Treleaven, 2019), automated decision-making and data welfare do not avoid friction (Dencik et al., 2018; Eubanks, 2018; Zarsky, 2015). Apart from the issue of explanatory power, problems of ethics and accountability (Ananny, 2016; Sandvig et al., 2016) – including the question of human agency concerning complex socio-technical systems (Kitchin, 2017; Velkova & Kaun, 2021) – have also been indicated as important challenges of automated decision-making.

Simultaneously, datafication is intricately linked to both the shifts in welfare provisions and the overall transformations of the welfare state. Namely, there are important shifts in the administration of welfare provision that emerge with digitalisation and identify how digital technologies, like algorithms, affect democracy. These shifts are often cited in professional contexts as marking the onset of a fourth industrial revolution (e.g. Schwab, 2016), which is founded on 'smart' digitalisation with the help of AI, algorithms and autonomous systems after mechanisation, mass production and computerisation (Schiølin, 2019). The larger implications of automated decision-making are premised on three shifts: First, a push towards automated decision-making and datafication of large parts of society, including the delegation of tasks to algorithms, AI and autonomous systems (Hintz et al., 2019; Kitchin, 2014; Mayer-Schönberger & Cukier, 2013; van Dijck, 2014); second, major changes in the organisation of the public sector that have been collectively described as the crisis of the welfare state (Castles, 2004); and, third, changes in civic engagement and participation (Buckingham, 2000; Conway, 2000; Milner, 2002; Putnam, 2001; Skocpol, 2003) that have been extensively addressed as a crisis of democracy since the early 2000s (Rosanvallon, 2008; Skocpol, 2003).

Besides, automated decision-making is intertwined with the transformation of the welfare state. Large-scale economic crises since the early 1970s have led to a shift in how welfare provision in Western democracy is organised (Bleses & Seeleib-Kaiser, 2004; Bonoli & Natali, 2012; Gilbert, 2002; Hemerijck, 2020). Often referred to as dismantling or transformation of the welfare state, a number of governments have privatised specific public services – including education, child and health care as well as the corrections and the media sector – and increasingly introduced the model of new public management to run public sector organisations with the objective of making them more efficient by implementing private sector management routines (Homburg et al., 2007). With processes of digitalisation and datafication, we are experiencing a shift towards a new regime of welfare provision that is intricately linked to digital infrastructures that result in new forms of control and support. This new welfare regime, which has been described as new public analytics (Yeung, 2023), is characterised by new forms of privatisation that not only take, for example, shape in new actors such as technology companies and coders entering the field of public administration but also emerge in the form of increased delegation and reliance on complex technological systems (Veale & Brass, 2019).

Andreassen et al. (2021) have previously highlighted important pillars of the ideal type of the data welfare state based on earlier arguments of the media welfare state proposed by Syvertsen and colleagues (2014). They argue that the data welfare state must be based on (1) justice and non-bias in processes of datafication; (2) decommodification, that is, freedom from commercial logic; (3) data diversity acknowledging different needs of citizens and residents; and (4) transparency on the datafication process providing sustainable and meaningful information for citizens and residents (p. 201). Extending this call for specific ideals that must guide the welfare state, we explore the current state of data welfare in terms of implementation, experiences and re-negotiations.

To map and explain the transformations of the welfare state in relation to introducing automated solutions and approaches in the public administration, our empirical focus is mainly on three countries – Estonia, Germany and Sweden, illustrating diverse types of welfare state regimes. Following and extending Esping-Andersen's (Esping-Andersen, 1990) typology of welfare state regimes, the chosen countries represent (a) a social democratic welfare state model, namely Sweden; (b) a corporatist–statist welfare state model, namely Germany; and (c) a post-socialist welfare state model, namely Estonia. In classifying welfare states, we distinguish between social democratic welfare states, which prioritise universal support, equality and decommodification of public services; corporatist–statist welfare states, rooted in historical guild systems, emphasising social class stratification; and post-socialist welfare models, combining liberal elements with competition-focused policies, albeit with variations.

These ideal types have faced critique, with some proposing alternative classifications, such as social democratic, conservative, liberal and radical welfare regimes. However, for the purposes of our study, we adhere to Esping-Andersen's original categorisation, including the post-socialist type, to analyse variations in attitudes towards automated decision-making in public administration. Furthermore, these three countries represent varying degrees of digitisation and automation within their welfare systems, each operating under distinct welfare regimes. This diversity allows us to discern the political underpinnings of these transformative processes.

This book's empirical foundation rests on a multifaceted analysis of automated decision-making within three welfare systems. Our data collection efforts included expert interviews with representatives from public agencies implementing automated decision-making as well as intermediaries such as digitalisation consultants and incubators. We also captured the citizen's viewpoint through a representative, self-administered survey conducted in Estonia, Germany and Sweden. The survey covered a range of variables, including experiences and attitudes towards algorithmic automation, awareness of data subject rights as defined by regulations like the General Data Protection Regulation and national laws, general data practices (including social media usage and information and communication technology literacy) and socio-demographics. Our quantitative analysis of these data illuminates overarching patterns in experiences and attitudes, providing a broad understanding of civic responses and expectations regarding automated decision-making in the welfare sector. Building upon this empirical foundation, the book conducts in-depth thematic analyses. These encompass practices related to navigating complex technological systems and the evolving roles within the welfare sector (implementation); the impact on citizens in terms of service quality, biases and justice (experiences); and avenues for resisting and influencing the transformation of the welfare state from the grassroots (resistance).

Based on empirically mapping, we elucidate the changes in these ideal types and examples of welfare state resulting from the integration of automated decision-making tools and practices. It covers shifts in both the conceptualisation and implementation of the welfare state, as well as the potential challenges these changes may pose. Divided into five interrelated chapters, the book maps the historical and intertwined transformations of the welfare provision and the history of computing (Chapter 1), the mundanisation and implementation of algorithmic public services as an outcome and process of social transformations in the welfare regimes (Chapter 2), the experiences of citizens and stakeholders in public administration, policy and industry in implementing the automated decision-making (Chapter 3), frictions of the data welfare and resulting resistances to automated decision-making (Chapter 4) and rethinking the welfare in the age of automation (Chapter 5.)

The first chapter, **Automating Public Services**, outlines the contours of the data welfare state across different welfare regimes. Going beyond merely mapping the extent to which the data welfare state has been established, we zoom in on the controversies around specific automation projects. We consider especially the experimental character of welfare automation that results in the fact that a majority of pilot studies and automation attempts are never fully implemented or scaled up. Automating welfare emerges hence as an ongoing practice and negotiation based on clear tensions between promises and reality. Here the data welfare state appears as an unfulfilled future promise that is often based on fundamental contradictions. This chapter also establishes the history of connecting ideas of the welfare state with technology and science in general, and history of computing in particular. Early on population statistics and registries were considered as an essential part of providing welfare through social engineering. Consequently, the automation within welfare services is not considered as radically new but as an extension of formative ideas of the welfare state. Drawing from three welfare state examples, Estonia, Germany and Sweden, we seek to both chart and elucidate the driving forces behind automation, considering historical developments in computing and the concept of the welfare state. This chapter explores the specific mechanisms that have contributed to the differentiation of the three welfare state models covered in this book: social democratic, corporatist–statist and post-socialist.

In the second chapter, **The Mundanisation of Algorithmic Public Services,** we follow the implementation of data-based public administration through several case studies, including the automation of benefit applications, AI applications developed by the employment services, algorithmic selection of e-residents, refugee relocation and automation of city transport. The focus is on mundane practices of sense-making by both civil servants and citizens in the process. We delve into the ways in which individuals relate to digital technologies for automation in their daily lives. This includes practices such as assigning human names to algorithms and tools used for robotic process automation, as well as treating these digital entities as if they were staff alongside human colleagues. This allows us to draw a picture of how emerging technology is integrated into everyday lives and hence made mundane until it blends into the background becoming invisible. This chapter engages with the question how non-technical experts relate to complex systems in their daily work developing mundane strategies of sense-making. This also includes shifts in the profession of case workers in the welfare sector and their changing tasks as well as self-perceptions.

The third chapter, **Experiences of Data Welfare,** focuses on the experiences of the data welfare state as it emerges for citizens that interact with automated systems, digital platforms and communicative AI (including chatbots) to interact with the public administration. This chapter draws primarily on a representative survey conducted in

2021 in Germany, Estonia and Sweden capturing experiences and attitudes towards the data welfare state by citizens. It furthermore engages with findings from focus group discussions with especially vulnerable groups and their experiences with the data welfare state. These include discussions of automated social services as well as services by the public employment agencies.

This chapter also explores the changing state–citizen relations from the citizens' perspective. It explores how the state and welfare provision is perceived as it is increasingly mediated through digital platforms and automated systems. The chapter presents a discussion of the ambivalent development of trust based on this mediation that is strengthened for certain groups while others increasingly distrust the state. The findings situated in the European context are contextualised through an international outlook of experiencing welfare automation beyond the Global North. This contextualisation makes clear that technological change is always situated in specific social, political and economic configurations.

The next chapter, **(Re-)Configuring Data Welfare,** explores forms of citizen activism to influence the outset of the data welfare state. This includes work by journalists, citizens and advocacy groups as well as unions who actively engage in the discussions around the advantages *and* the dark side of the data welfare state. The effort of these groups is very much focused on establishing the data welfare state as a political rather than a merely administrative issue. Based on the analysis, this chapter develops ways ahead for the data welfare state discussing aspirations and potential alternative futures that move beyond the emphasis of efficiency. The chapter also pushes the boundaries of early critiques of the data welfare and presents answers to the question 'What can be done?' beyond values of transparency and accountability. Ultimately, the chapter reinforces the assumption that data welfare is fundamentally about how we want to live our lives together in societies that allow for human flourishing and prosperity.

The book ends with concluding remarks about whether and in what ways we need to rethink welfare in the age of automation. This last chapter is programmatic and outlines a manifest for engaged scholarship that contributes to a data welfare state that allows a good life for all and that has an explicit normative grounding in the needs and rights of citizens for human flourishing. The chapter provides concrete advice on how to retool the automation of welfare and the data welfare state. The book ends with bold visions for how the data welfare state could and should be organised differently.

References

Agar, J. (2003). *The government machine: A revolutionary history of the computer.* MIT Press.
Allardt, E. (1975). *Att ha, att älska, att vara. Om välfärden i Norden.* Argos.
Andreassen, R., Kaun, A., & Nikunen, K. (2021). Fostering the data welfare state: A Nordic perspective on datafication. *Nordicom Review, 42*(2), 207–223.
Ananny, M. (2016). Toward an ethics of algorithms: Convening, observation, probability, and timeliness. *Science, Technology & Human Values, 41*(1), 93–117.

Bastani, A. (2019). *Fully automated luxury communism*. Verso Books.
Bleses, P., & Seeleib-Kaiser, M. (2004). *The dual transformation of the German welfare state*. Palgrave Macmillan.
Benanav, A. (2020). A world without work? *Dissent, 67*(4), 45–52.
Bonoli, G., & Natali, D. (2012). The politics of the "new" welfare states: Analyzing reforms in Western Europe. In G. Bonoli & D. Natali (Eds.), *the politics of the new welfare state* (pp. 3–20). Oxford University Press.
Buckingham, D. (2000). *The making of citizens. Young people, news, and politics*. Routledge.
Castles, F. (2004). The future of the welfare state: Crisis myths and crisis realities. *International Journal of Health Services, 32*. https://doi.org/10.2190/GJ9M-WUGX-DMJ2-35PA
Conway, M. (2000). *Political participation in the United States*. Congressional Quarterly Inc.
Dencik, L., Hintz, A., Redden, J., & Warne, H. (2018, December 1). *Data scores as Governance: Investigating uses of citizen scoring in public services project report* [Monograph]. Open Society Foundations. https://orca.cardiff.ac.uk/id/eprint/117517/
Dencik, L., & Kaun, A. (2020). Datafication and the welfare state. *Global Perspectives, 1*(1), 12912.
Engin, Z., & Treleaven, P. (2019). Algorithmic government: Automating public services and supporting civil servants in using data science technologies. *The Computer Journal, 62*(3), 448–460. https://doi.org/10.1093/comjnl/bxy082
Esping-Andersen, G. (1990). *The three worlds of welfare capitalism*. Princeton University Press.
Eubanks, V. (2018). *Automating inequality: How high-tech tools profile, police, and punish the poor* (1st ed.). St. Martin's Press.
Fourcade, M. (2021). Ordinal citizenship. *British Journal of Sociology, 72*(2), 154–173. https://doi.org/10.1111/1468-4446.12839
Frey, C. B. (2019). *The technology trap: Capital, labor, and power in the age of automation*. Princeton University Press.
Gilbert, N. (2002). *Transformation of the welfare state: The silent surrender of public responsibility*. Oxford University Press.
Hemerijck, A. (2020). Social investment as a policy paradigm. In M. R. Busemeyer, C. de la Porte, J. L. Garritzmann, & E. Pavolini (Eds.), *The future of the social investment state* (pp. 10–27). Routledge.
Hintz, A., Dencik, L., & Wahl-Jorgensen, K. (2019). *Digital citizenship in a datafied society*. Polity Press.
Högberg, C. (2023). Big data: Automated decision-making in public policy. In M. van Gerven, C. Rothmayr, & K. Schubert (Eds.), *Encyclopedia of public policy*. Springer. https://doi.org/10.1007/978-3-030-90434-0_59-1
Högberg, C., Larsson, S., & Lång, K. (2023). Anticipating artificial intelligence in mammography screening: Views of Swedish breast radiologists. *BMJ Health & Care Informatics, 30*(1).
Homburg, V., Pollitt, C., & Thiel, S. (2007). *New public management in Europe: Adaptation and alternatives* (p. 229). https://doi.org/10.1057/9780230625365
Jakobsson, P., Lindell, J., & Stiernstedt, F. (2023). Normative foundations of media welfare: Perspectives from the Nordic countries. *Media, Culture & Society, 45*(2), 305–322. https://doi.org/10.1177/01634437221111914

Kennedy, H. (2016). *Post, mine, repeat: Social media data mining becomes ordinary*. Springer.
Kitchin, R. (2014). *The data revolution: Big data, open data, data infrastructures & their consequences*. SAGE.
Kitchin, R. (2017). Thinking critically about and researching algorithms. *Information, Communication & Society, 20*(1), 14–29. https://doi.org/10.1080/1369118X.2016.1154087
Lindert, P. H. (2004). *Growing public: Volume 1, the story: Social spending and economic growth since the eighteenth century* (Vol. 1). Cambridge University Press.
Mayer-Schönberger, V., & Cukier, K. (2013). *Big data: A revolution that will transform how we live, work and think*. John Murray.
Milner, H. (2002). *Civic literacy: How informed citizens make democracy work*. University Press of New England.
Mosco, V. (2017). *Becoming digital: Toward a post-internet society*. Emerald Publishing Limited.
O'Neil, C. (2016). *Weapons of math destruction: How big data increases inequality and threatens democracy* (1st ed.). Crown.
Polanyi, K. (1944). *The great transformation*. Rhinehart.
Putnam, R. D. (2001). *Bowling alone: The collapse and revival of American community*. Simon & Schuster.
Redden, J., Dencik, L., & Warne, H. (2020). Datafied child welfare services: Unpacking politics, economics and power, *Policy Studies, 41*(5), 507–526. https://doi.org/10.1080/01442872.2020.1724928
Rosanvallon, P. (2008). *Counter-democracy: Politics in the Age of Distrust*. Cambridge University Press.
Ruckenstein, M. (2023). *The feel of algorithms*. University of California Press.
Sandvig, C., Hamilton, K., Karahalios, K., & Langbort, C. (2016). When the algorithm itself is a racist: Diagnosing ethical harm in the basic components of software. *International Journal of Communication, 10*, 4972–4990.
Schiølin, K. (2019). Revolutionary dreams: Future essentialism and the sociotechnical imaginary of the fourth industrial revolution in Denmark. *Social Studies of Science*, 1–25.
Schwab, K. (2016). *The fourth industrial revolution*. Random House.
Skocpol, T. (2003). *Diminished democracy. From membership to management in American civic life*. University of Oklahoma Press.
Sophus Lai, S., Andelsman, V., & Flensburg, S. (2023). Datafied school life: The hidden commodification of digital learning. *Learning, Media and Technology*. https://doi.org/10.1080/17439884.2023.2219063
Spielkamp, M. (2019, January). *Automating society: Taking stock of automated decision-making in the EU. BertelsmannStiftung Studies 2019* [Other]. http://aei.pitt.edu/102677/
Syvertsen, T., Enli, G., Mjøs, O. J., & Moe, H. (2014). *The media welfare state: Nordic media in the digital era*. University of Michigan Press. https://doi.org/10.3998/nmw.12367206.0001.001
van Dijck, J. (2014). Datafication, dataism and dataveillance: Big data between scientific paradigm and ideology. *Surveillance and Society, 12*(2), 197–208.

van Toorn, G., & Scully, J. L. (2023). Unveiling algorithmic power: Exploring the impact of automated systems on disabled people's engagement with social services. *Disability & Society*. https://doi.org/10.1080/09687599.2023.2233684

Veale, M., & Brass, I. (2019). *Administration by algorithm? Public management meets public sector machine learning*. In K. Yeung & M. Lodge (Eds.), *Algorithmic regulation*. Oxford University Press. Available at SSRN: https://ssrn.com/abstract=3375391

Velkova, J., & Kaun, A. (2021). Algorithmic resistance: Media practices and the politics of repair. *Information, Communication & Society, 24*(4), 523–540. https://doi.org/10.1080/1369118X.2019.1657162

Wajcman, J. (2017). Automation: Is it really different this time? *British Journal of Sociology, 68*(1), 119–127.

Williams, R. (1976). *Keywords: A vocabulary of culture and society*. Fontana Press.

Yeung, K. (2023). The new public analytics as an emerging paradigm in public sector administration. *27*(2), Article 2. https://doi.org/10.5334/tilr.303

Zarsky, T. (2015). The trouble with algorithmic decisions: An analytic road map to examine efficiency and fairness in automated and opaque decision making. *Science, Technology, and Human Values, 41*(1), 118–132.

1
Evolving Data Welfare State

Scene 1 - 1700: The Orphanage Hospitals. In the dusky alleys of 18th-century London, the flickering glow of gas lamps cast long shadows on cobblestone streets. The year is 1705, and amidst the squalor, a beacon of hope emerges – the doors of St. Anne's Orphanage Hospital swing open to welcome destitute children. Inside, the air is laced with the scent of musty wood and echoes with the hushed whispers of caretakers attending to the orphans. In a dimly lit corner, a matronly figure cradles an infant, abandoned and left at the mercy of the harsh streets. The flickering candlelight reveals a makeshift crib, fashioned from weathered wood, offering a semblance of solace to the abandoned child. St. Anne's stands as a testament to the era's nascent efforts at providing welfare, though rudimentary, for those without familial refuge.

Scene 2 - 1950: Old Age Insurance. Fast forward to the post-war optimism of 1953. The scene shifts to the bustling offices of a government building, where the notion of societal care extends beyond the young. The advent of old age insurance unfolds as workers, now greyed by time, navigate paperwork and bureaucratic processes. The air is thick with the scent of freshly typed documents and the distant hum of typewriters. At a wooden desk, an ageing clerk guides an elderly man through the intricacies of the newly established old-age insurance program. The clinking of coins, now replaced by the swiping of social security cards, echoes the shift in societal responsibility toward caring for the elderly. It's a moment of transition – a step towards recognizing the collective duty to ensure a dignified life for those who have weathered the years.

Scene 3 - 2030: Sickness Insurance. Zooming ahead to a technologically advanced 2030, the setting unfolds in a sleek and modern insurance agency. The hum of artificial intelligence algorithms fills the air, as holographic interfaces display health coverage options. In stark contrast to the orphanage and the bureaucratic offices of yesteryears, this scene epitomises the evolution of societal care. A young woman, battling a chronic illness, sits across from a virtual insurance agent, discussing personalised coverage plans. The exchange is marked by the digitised rustle of policy documents and the soft glow of holographic projections. The contours of the future are shaped by a commitment to providing comprehensive sickness insurance, acknowledging the nuanced health needs of individuals.

In this first chapter, we prepare the groundwork for our examination of the data welfare state and not only its far-reaching effects on but also the tight interrelatedness with social changes that take its expression increasingly in public service automation and datafication. We provide a brief overview of the historical progress of the data welfare state and the underlying social mechanisms that propel this transformative process. We provide an overview of the state of the data welfare state across various welfare regimes. Our approach goes beyond mere assessment of the extent to which the data welfare state has been implemented; instead, we delve into the controversies surrounding specific automation projects. We pay particular attention to the experimental nature of welfare automation, which often leads to many pilot studies and automation attempts often being not fully implemented, scaled up or their reception among real user groups being tested. This perspective frames automating welfare as an ongoing practice and negotiation marked by clear tensions between promised outcomes and actual realities. In this context, the data welfare state frequently appears as an unrealised future promise, often rooted in fundamental contradictions. The welfare state automation is not merely the result or outcome of historical social transformation processes but is inherently an ongoing process of social change. Historically, welfare state automation has emerged within interconnected processes of digitisation, computation and the continual evolution of welfare ideas. These processes are further elaborated upon in this chapter.

Empirically, this chapter is based on extensive investigations of welfare automation projects in three countries: Sweden, Estonia and Germany. These countries are selected for their relevance to the global context of the data welfare state and their representation of diverse historical models of welfare provision. This diversity makes them intriguing cases for examining the interconnected processes of digital transformation and welfare state concepts. The chapter introduces the concept of the data welfare state as a form of social transformation that will be the central focus of this book. It draws on prior research in the fields of welfare, critical data and algorithm studies, digital transformations and the history of computing to provide a historically and theoretically grounded introduction to the concept of the data welfare state. The central theme explored in understanding the emergence of the data welfare state is the notion of contradictions and tensions arising from technologically mediated changes, which have become increasingly apparent in recent decades. These contradictions, particularly in the context of automation, reveal the inherent frictions within welfare systems operating under late capitalism, a phenomenon that has become more pronounced in recent years. Automation technologies are seen as a means of highlighting these contradictions while placing them within the lived experiences of case workers and citizens.

This chapter provides an overview of key historical developments and underlying social mechanisms that have driven and elucidated the growing automation of public services. It also underscores a notable gap in previous research on social datafication: an explanation of social changes associated with automation.

Consequently, this chapter introduces a theoretical framework aimed at elucidating the disparities between automation promises and outcomes in the context of welfare, shedding light on why ongoing negotiations have resulted in tensions within the welfare state.

Public Service Automation and Datafication in Driving Social Change

In this section, we embark on a comprehensive exploration of public service automation, examining its role as a catalyst for profound social change. Our journey takes us through the fundamental transformations in the delivery and experience of public services in the digital age. At the same time, we challenge the static view of welfare automation and instead embrace it as a dynamic agent – a force that can actively contribute to making social changes. We contend that welfare automation does not solely emerge from deliberate efforts to enhance administrative efficiency or the unintended consequences of applying digital technologies in welfare provision. Rather, it should be seen as an integral component of ever-evolving social transformation processes. These intricate processes encompass shifts in underlying technological infrastructures, interconnected transformations in social norms and values linked to welfare and the evolving principles and conceptions of the welfare state.

We introduce a framework for understanding social transformation as a viable approach to unravel the intricacies and tensions between the realms of well-being and datafication. This framework equips us to navigate the complex historical processes interwoven with the automation of welfare. It enables us to elucidate both anticipated, deliberate social changes and unforeseen disruptions – that will be exemplified below – within this continuous process of transformation. These disruptions may yield potential risks, and harms, as well as tensions and frictions that require exploration and analysis.

Inspired from the theoretical and methodological framework of social transformations (Archer, 1995; Archer & Maccarini, 2021; Masso, Lauristin, et al., 2020), we consider welfare automation and datafication as intertwined processes of transitions in digital computing technologies, on the one hand, and principles and practices providing social welfare in the societies, on the other hand. We assume that the social changes towards the implementation of automated tools in the public sector and the principles and practices of the welfare state can be characterised not only by gradual changes but they are also intrinsically part of the broader fundamental social transformations that societies constantly go through. This process of change means that previously dominating ways of executing public administration, underlying technical understandings of processes of providing welfare services, underlying aided computational tools are replaced and expanded with new practices and understandings. We do not assume that the movement to 'old' and 'new' practices necessarily entails quantitative shifts like ensuring higher levels of social welfare in the societies, or qualitative shifts like introducing completely new ways of understanding the welfare state. Instead, we propose that emerging interrelated changes in social computing and welfare provisions are raising questions about, agreements in or conflicts about norms of security, safety and transparency, or values of justice, sustainability and equality, which can lay the foundation for certain new welfare automation practices and data-based welfare state models. These changes towards data-based organisational culture have also been called 'data acculturation' – critically self-reflexive learning through data as a form of change in organisations and among data professionals (Masso, Männiste, & Calzati, 2023). For example, a data expert working in a public sector organisation emphasised in one of our studies:

> I used data for reorganising management. I gave up work plans and traditional plans. (…) Managers must immediately get an online overview of how things are (…) I taught managers to ask which of the trends is better? (data expert working in public sector).

In these expert interviews, we examined in detail how data experts working in various sectors perceive the transition to data-based decision-making, including their opinions and daily practices related to it. The following quote vividly illustrates the cultural shift occurring within organisations. In this case, change in organizational data culture was initiated and led by a single data analyst, a self-described data evangelist, who introduced the benefits of a data-based approach to the management and the entire organisation.

The social transformation approach we rely on in this book originates from the social morphogenesis introduced by Margaret Archer (2010, 1995). In prior projects we have similarly worked with the social transformation framework, for example, in the context of examining rapid and fundamental social changes in the politics, society and economics in the East and Central European countries (Masso, Lauristin, et al., 2020). The approach has now been moved into the field of algorithmic approaches in a wide array of social domains and the related challenges to humans in these applications (Archer & Maccarini, 2021; Braun et al., 2021; Donati, 2021). We here, however, make a first attempt to apply this theoretical–methodological framework for mapping and examining the social changes related to welfare state automation and datafication. Whereas some prior powerful approaches to digital social transformations have foremost grasped the complex systemic and macro-level social transitions (Kanger, 2016; Perez, 2010), other approaches have emphasized the key role of human agency – initiatives and actions of the engaged humans (Kennedy & Moss, 2015), with their values, understandings and cognitions expressed publicly, as a driving force of social transformations that this automation has led to. We suggest combining these two approaches. We argue that combining these prior valuable macro- and micro-level, systemic and agency-related approaches is necessary to better understand and explain the complex, multilevel and networked processes that have led not only to efficient and effective prosperity services but also to tensions and frictions in public sector automation. Of course, the social transformation approach we are relying on here is not free of limitations, since it only provides us an explanatory theoretical framework, which does not allow us to give always answers about the causes, driving forces and mechanisms, how and why certain changes in public administration, automation and welfare systems happen and why they lead to tensions and frictions in certain cases. This theoretical framework, when filled with practical and empirical content, could be used for mapping and explaining the interrelated change processes in experiences, practices, norms and values within the public administration institutions, and in society at large, which creates the context for the implementation of these applications.

The key elements of the theoretical–methodological framework we rely on involve three key elements – structure (S), culture (C) and agency (A) – that are vital for every social change process related to public sector practices, welfare provisions and implementing calculative devices and methods in these areas (SAC principle, see Figure 1.1). Based on this framework, the primary driving force behind social transformations is the diverse array of human actors, as depicted in Figure 1.1 (agency in the figure), called in the data studies also triple agency (Masso et al., 2022; Masso et al., 2020). First, these multiple agencies include experts such as engineers and designers responsible for the development of data models, as well as team managers and governance experts who guide the development processes, on the one hand. Additionally, citizens play a critical role by contributing the necessary data for model training or by being end-users of the solutions created to address societal challenges. Furthermore, human actors extend to private and public sector institutions, civil society organisations, countries and international associations. In essence, these human agents are central figures in serving not only as recipients but also as initiators of the social transformations catalysed by automating the welfare state. Third, besides these multiple stakeholders, the quantitative calculations, algorithms and machine learning models implemented tend to always have, at least to some degree in any case, its' performativity – the unintended consequences (both negative and positive) that the developers and managers may not have foreseen, or in other words, 'its own life' of functioning and practicing.

All the agencies must adhere to established structural processes, as illustrated in Figure 1.1 (structural changes in Figure 1.1). These processes encompass various elements, including data infrastructure (e.g. data access) and compliance with norms and regulations (e.g. guidelines for designing machine learning models). Furthermore, their actions are deeply intertwined with the surrounding cultural processes (depicted as 'cultural changes' in Figure 1.1). As a result, when developing models, they draw upon ideas, values and norms. These ever-evolving structural and cultural conditions inform, initiate and prepare individuals, organisations and societies for change. These conditions, however, are in a constant state of flux. This ongoing transformation primarily occurs through social and cultural interactions, resulting in continuous and

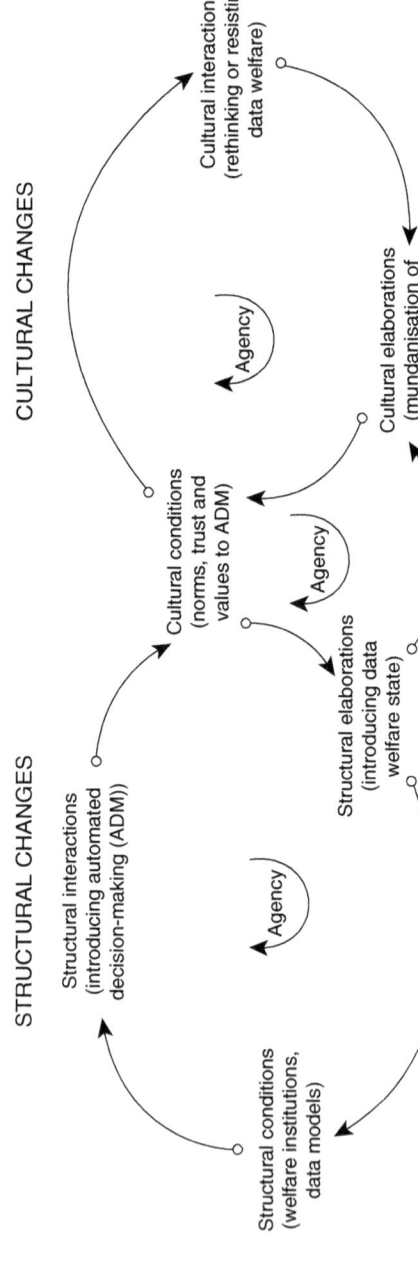

Figure 1.1 Transformative Mechanisms of Welfare Automation

Note: Authors' figure based on SAC idea (S-structure, A-agency, C-culture, as introduced by Archer, 2013).

all-encompassing changes. These transitions extend to data infrastructure, encompassing the introduction, design and adoption of new machine learning techniques to address everyday challenges. These transformations lead to shifts in cultural values and social norms that shape the development of applications within specific institutional settings and the implementation of data models. However, one of the challenges in introducing automated and data-based solutions is that these shifts do not happen simultaneously but might be expressed with varying speed at different points in time, with shifting intensity and scale. For example, as one of data experts working in public sector in one of our studies expressed (Männiste & Masso, 2020):

> And quite often it is here rather like educating like I have been in this organization for three years. ... I just walked around and introduced what data analytics is, why it is used, and where it can be useful. Distributing this kind of culture so that we could have a data-based organization (data expert working in public sector).

This interview demonstrates that varying levels of readiness for a data culture shift can also exist within an organisation, where change initiators and implementers may be individual 'data pioneers'. Their effective and extensive efforts in explaining and training others in both data analytical techniques and data-driven management principles (such as the benefits of real-time dashboards for quick decision-making) have helped the organisation achieve fundamental changes (e.g. real-time prevention of and response to traffic accidents).

Therefore, it's crucial to recognise that the timing of these changes varies significantly. Some shifts are short-term, spanning from a few months to a few years, such as during the development and implementation of data and computational models in public sector institutions. Meanwhile, others fall into the medium-term category, extending from a few years to a decade, encompassing technological innovations like the development of explainable machine learning models. The most challenging changes to trace are social transformations, which become evident through scrutiny of welfare state processes over extended periods, sometimes spanning decades, or through comparisons between different stages of change historically, such as comparing practices of automation of welfare across countries, domains and organisations. Behind the long-term nature of these changes are the necessary cultural shifts in values and norms, the negotiation, adaptation and modification of which is a time-consuming process. One of the examples of such 'delayed' transformations is what is happening in public administration organisations, where varying organisational cultures, including those with fonder of implementing data-based solutions, and those being somewhat more cautious or directly expressing resistances to these innovations, exist side by side in organisations. One of the examples for such 'double movements' (Männiste & Masso, 2020; Masso, Männiste, & Calzati, 2023) is presented below:

> The everyday work of advisers is very intense, and they just do not have time, and we also, unfortunately, do not have an analyst's position (register data, forced migration). We do not use [algorithms] (...) We have separate people who are directly involved with data (data expert from public sector organisation).

This example illustrates that the manifestation of social changes, as well as understanding and explaining these processes, is especially difficult since these elements are not linearly or causally related, but relational (Archer, 2010, 1995; Lauristin et al., 2017). It means that emerging novel structural conditions like introducing new calculation methods (e.g. machine learning, large language models, generative AI) do not automatically lead to using these solutions in public sector institutions and new ways of providing services in public administration like automating welfare provisions, on the one hand. These technical innovations do not lead necessarily to shifts in social norms, values and trust to the increasing use of automated solutions in the public sector organisations and consequently to shifts in state-citizen relations. Instead, technological innovations often tend to manifest or be related with reverse and intermittent movements (e.g. skipping some phases). Such interwoven and multi-speed movements can lead to automation success stories as well as disruptions and even conflicts or public scandals, as the examples in the following chapters vividly illustrate (see Chapters 3 and 4).

Therefore, these feedback loops between structural and cultural conditions, structural and cultural interactions and structural and cultural elaborations (arrows in Figure 1.1), as initiated, led and applied by the active and multiple actors, are not always leading to positive futures like improved qualities in assuring social well-being and strengthening democracy – for example, supporting democratic values such as inclusion and justice, or encouraging citizens readiness and participation co-creating the data-based solutions. To the contrary, these interrelations between structural and cultural processes might also lead to negative changes like automating inequalities, injustice, legitimising and reconstructing the prior power hierarchies in the societies, as several prior studies and empirical examples on applying datafied solutions, algorithms and automation in the public administration have clearly shown (Couldry & Mejias, 2019; Eubanks, 2018; O'Neil, 2016; Taylor, 2017). We also assume that situations are possible where feedback loops take place in such a way that the same structural conditions and cultural assumptions continue, be it for example resistance to new principles, practices, values and norms, which is why the introduction of computational methods does not always lead to changes in the welfare system. As the next interviewees with data and healthcare experts illustrate (Masso et al., 2022) (see also Chapter 4 on Resisting Data Welfare):

> The advantage [of automation in health care] is technological advancement in our health sector... Technology has the capacity to improve quality of care. (expert in the field of health care)

> It [automated solutions] may not diagnose early, or it may misdiagnose and result in false-positive; and if these biases are there, if the diagnosis is not right, then a lot of things can go wrong. (data expert)

These interviews were conducted with medical and data experts, as well as parents, to gather feedback on the suitability of using artificial intelligence solutions in the healthcare sector. Specifically, the focus was on a mobile application developed to detect deviations in infant cries and, consequently, the risks for serious health conditions. The examples vividly illustrate that the welfare systems, countries and cases are not independent or evolve separately from each other in nation states but relate individual countries to each other on a European and global scale. For example, Estonia has had tight historical connections with Sweden and Germany. Therefore, when discussing the development and building up its welfare system in beginning of 1990s after the dissolution of the Soviet Union, the well-established welfare state models like those in Germany and Sweden have been used not only as potential examples but also as role models. However, as expressed in the public speeches, interviews and political discussions, key persons initiating these changes saw quite quickly that there is an urgent need to find new and differently contextualised solutions to avoid path dependencies – the events and experiences as a country occupied by the Russian authorities for almost 50 years (see e.g. Vihalemm et al., 2017), which is why there was a significant lag in modern economic and political processes compared to Western countries, potentially constraining the later developments of the country. The way out from these path dependencies, finding its own new way, was in the Estonian case the inventing, introduction and implementation of the digital state.

In the next chapters, we explain the ways how the feedback loops in the social transformations in public sector have led to mundanisation of the algorithmic public services, how the experiences of automation have developed and expressed and how values and norms related to automation have supported this change processes, and alternatively, how the tensions and frictions are expressed, as a 'failed' forms of public sector transformations.

The Evolution of the Data Welfare State: A Historical Perspective

The shift towards welfare datafication and automation has not unfolded in isolation; rather, it has been intricately intertwined with structural and cultural processes. These structural processes that this chapter addresses are evolutions in the welfare state model, on the one hand, and the introduction and shifts in the implementation of computational approaches in the public administration, on the other hand. All of these processes of change have been shaped, developed or resisted against by active stakeholders. To gain a deeper understanding of the dynamics and fundamental and intertwined aspects of these developments, it is imperative that we delve into the historical processes that have mutually influenced and driven change in the context of automation. Therefore, in the following section, we examine key milestones and technological advancements that have shaped the modern welfare landscape and that are building the cornerstones for the data welfare state.

The central claim we make here is that at least two main historical processes of change that have been driving the emergence of the data welfare state – the implementation of computing infrastructure and the evolution of the idea of welfare state itself (see Figure 1.2). We suggest that the move towards a data welfare state (Dencik & Kaun, 2020; Esping-Andersen, 1990; Larsson & Haldar, 2021; Oorschot et al., 2008; Pan, 2020) is tightly intertwined with the computational turn and history of computing (Bodmer, 2021; Desrosières, 1998; Halpern, 2015; Kang, 2023; Morley, 2013), including the recent developments in multimodal or machine learning (e.g. Hitzler & Sarker, 2022; Kline et al., 2022; Mai et al., 2023). Although the emergence of and discussion on the welfare state ideas intensified after the second world war and in relation to the (re) building up the economy and the economic growth, the initial ideas extend back at least to the 18th century. Building orphanages in England in 1741 is one of these examples. However, during these centuries, the ideas of welfare and the understandings on the welfare state ideals have changed significantly, varying during time periods, countries and institutional settings (see Figure 1.2). Similarly, the current ideas of automation have its grounds in the histories of measuring and calculations and automation. Introducing the first computer algorithm by Ada Lovelace or using punch cards for mechanical computers are some of the examples. Therefore, to understand the emergence of the data welfare state, we need to see these processes, evolutions and transformations in these two domains – welfare and computing as being tightly interrelated, complementing and feeding each other.

Based on these processes, we can distinguish at least three stages of change in the interactions of the evolution of welfare ideas and developments of computing – (1) emergence of the initial ideas of welfare and computing, (2) infrastructural and institutional transformations and (3) evolution, crystallisation of the data welfare ideas as well as resistances to it. During the first stage, the initial ideas of welfare state and institutions, the need for ensuring the welfare services for the population to assure the basic economic and social security, have been emerging. Besides, the first institutions providing the welfare services were established, and initial grounds for the modern social policy were formulated. However, the ideas, policies and institutions of welfare were not yet widely spread, and the ideas and ideals of the welfare state were not yet taken its root; instead, the discussions on what the modern social policy ideals should address were widely prevalent.

In the second stage, the more fundamental institutional transformations were happening, foremost around the middle of 20th century, including the infrastructural shifts like introducing first electronic computers and the start of the commercialisation of computers, that gave grounds for wider spread of those technologies among citizens, but also in public administration institutions. On the other hand, the welfare state ideas

EVOLVING DATA WELFARE STATE

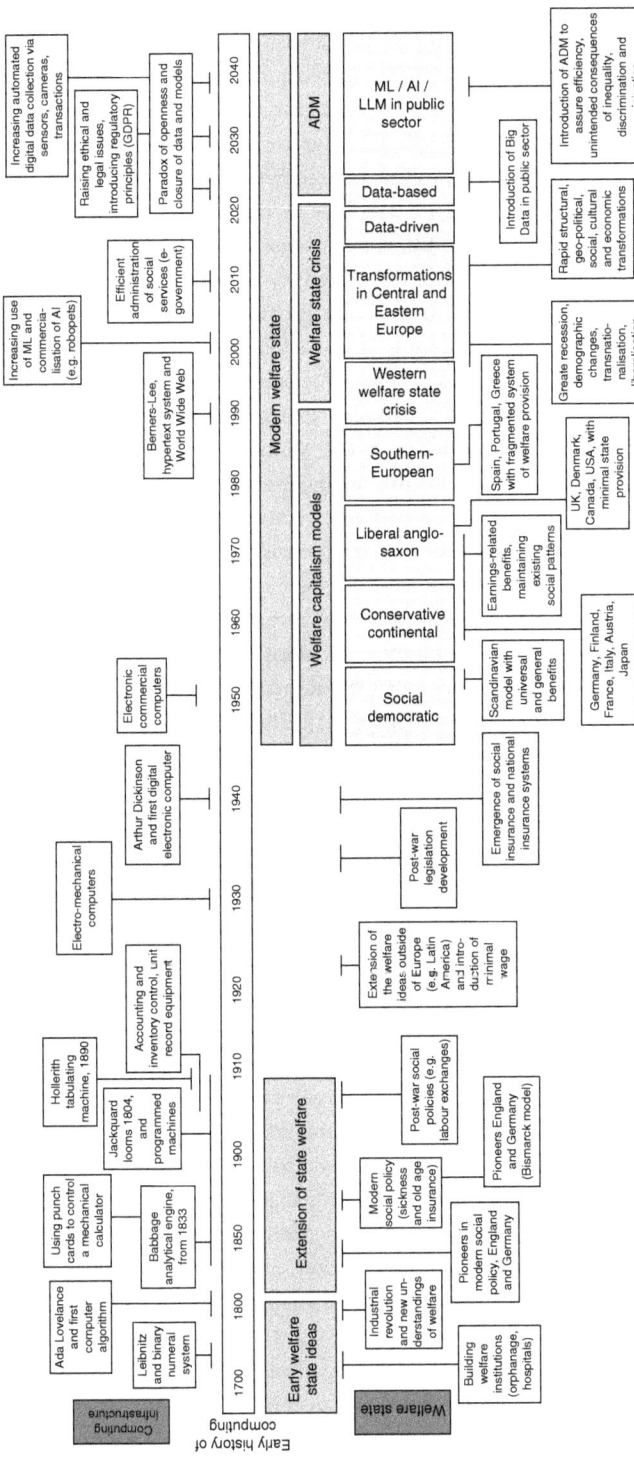

Figure 1.2 Historical Foundations of Public sector Automation

Source: Author's figure.

were made through significant transformations, so that the initial ideas became not only more widespread but also institutionalised and a significant part of the democratic states. Several examples characterise such mundanisation of the welfare state ideals, like introducing the insurance systems, developing the necessary legislation, or introducing institutions like orphanages. However, these developments took in reality somewhat different forms, ending up with different welfare models, as indicated in the figure.

The third stage could be conditionally named as the emergence of a data welfare state. From the welfare perspective, this stage is characterised by needs for assuring the efficiency in the public administration and providing necessary services, after some decades long search for solutions to the welfare state crisis and new models for responding to the challenges in the context of population growth and ageing globally. Initiatives like increasing use of varied data sources and electronic services have been introduced, after and in parallel with the shifts in digitalisation and computing. Temporally, geographically and institutionally, the variations could be characterised by shifts from data-driven forms of governance, where data served as a normative foundation and the primary means for managing decision-making processes. On the other hand, later developments, such as data-based and data-informed approaches, used data as a source for knowledge creation, with a greater emphasis on the role of humans in mediating and being responsible for these decisions. However, as we also have seen from history, the mundanisation process of the automated welfare state takes a longer time period and is still happening (see Figure 2.1). Therefore, there are both examples of mundanisation and signs of resistance, which are explained in more detail in Chapter 2 using specific domains and institutions as examples.

However, setting the exact time limits of these phases is not very easy, nor is it absolutely necessary in the context of this book. In this case we rather emphasise the great variability in these developments from country to country and the dynamic evolutionary processes and mechanisms driving these shifts. Although this book focuses on the European context and examples, these developments have been significantly influenced by what is happening in different countries (e.g. the invention of the Hollerith tabulating machine in the United States, using the punch cards, to speed up the population counting during the national census). However, despite this, we show in this book that even within Europe, based on three examples, Estonia, Germany, and Sweden, variations are important in both temporal and geographical perspectives, but also within the countries in regard of the citizens readiness and trust to automation.

Indeed, the intertwined historical processes that have given rise to and transitioned the technical computing infrastructure and evolving concepts of social welfare and welfare state have not occurred in isolation. In addition to these central transformations, broader societal changes encompassing structural and cultural conditions, the economy, politics, people's lifestyles, values and social norms are concurrently unfolding (Archer & Maccarini, 2021; Braun et al., 2021; Donati, 2021). As such, our central proposition is that the rapid digital transformations (Abolhassan, 2017; Glasze & Dammann, 2021; Heinrich, 2015; Karatzogianni et al., 2016; Kempeneer & Heylen,

2023; Mergel et al., 2019; Süssenguth, 2015), marked by the introduction of novel technological infrastructures like large-scale data, algorithmic approaches and implementing machine learning, based on these data, have been occurring within intricate interrelationships.

Algorithmic automation, within the context of the welfare state, can be viewed as both a continuation and an emergence of processes observed in other domains, such as the digitalisation of society (Athina Karatzogianni et al., 2016; Fuchs, 2015; Gates, 2019), the datafication of everyday life (Dalton et al., 2016; Kitchin, 2014; Masso, Tiidenberg, et al., 2020b; Schäfer & Van Es, 2017) and the platformisation of the economy and work (Masso et al., 2024., Van Dijck et al., 2018; Egbert, 2019; Poell et al., 2019). In essence, automation could be seen as a particular subtype of digital transformation in the public sector, characterised by familiar dynamics – those involving progress towards prosperity and well-being, as well as periods of stasis and disruption. These positive transformations manifest in various ways, including increased efficiency and effectiveness (Larsson & Haldar, 2021; Karppi, 2018; Lowrie, 2018), with the aspiration of achieving faster, more transparent and equitable decision-making. Automation can also inadvertently contribute to the legitimisation of social inequality (Eubanks, 2018; O'Neil, 2016).

While automation shares commonalities with societal, political and economic transformations, it also introduces distinctive elements specific to the welfare state. We propose that this distinctiveness is closely tied to the process of datafication – the increasingly intricate integration of everyday life, welfare provisions, state operations and public administration with quantified decision-making processes. Initially, such widespread use of data in evidence-based decision-making within public sector organisations, often referred to as data-driven governance (Bennett & Lyon, 2019; Dencik et al., 2019; Pentland, 2013; Masso, Männiste, & Calzati, 2023; Masso, Tiidenberg, et al., 2020a), held promise for more objective and efficient governance. This was particularly evident in the early stages of datafication, as shown in Figure 1.2 (circa, 2010).

However, as datafied and automated tools become more prevalent in public administration, several drawbacks emerged, including issues of data misuse and automation-driven inequality and algorithmic injustice, besides legal questions related to protection of personal data and assuring privacy. This prompted a heightened focus on ethical considerations. Consequently, a shift occurred from the previously dominant data-driven decision-making models, where data, measurements and indicators were assumed to hold a monopoly on truth and ensure the efficient functioning of the state. Instead, data-informed or data-based decision-making processes gained prominence (Drechsler, 2019; Haardörfer, 2019; Masso, Männiste, & Calzati, 2023; Masso, Tiidenberg, et al., 2020a). The latter approach emphasises the active involvement of human experts in decision-making, with algorithmic tools serving as complementary aids in the daily work led by humans. Additionally, alternative forms of governance that advocate decision-making without solely relying on data and numbers (Drechsler, 2019) were suggested as critical alternatives to address the challenges associated with the implementation of datafied decision-making in public administration.

These unique processes of change play a pivotal role in shaping the evolution of automation, particularly within the context of public sector institutions. These distinctive changes, aimed at advancing data welfare, have given rise to a dominant paradox that we call the 'paradox of openness and closure'. The paradox of data openness describes a phenomenon seen in public administration, where there is a growing commitment to enhancing knowledge creation through data collection, utilisation and sharing. While paradoxes of closure and openness can be similarly observed in other specific domains, such as forced migration (Schlüter et al., 2019) – where migration satisfies labour needs but is perceived as a threat to cultural identity – we assert that it is particularly prominent in the context of open government data and public sector automation. Despite the extensive scholarly attention given to the automation process (Carlson, 2018; Engin & Treleaven, 2019; Kaun et al., 2023; Larsson & Haldar, 2021), the openness paradox – essential for understanding why digital transformations aimed at increasing automation have at times been more successful – remains a notable area of focus. This paradox is especially visible in Estonia, that has gone through significant improvements, and exemplified in next extracts with data experts (Masso, Männiste, & Calzati, 2023):

> But we cannot have this data. The bank does not share... once we almost had an agreement with the bank, but it failed because they were afraid that maybe something would not be following their economic interest, comes from it... (data expert from public sector organisation)

> Includes many interesting databases, such as census data, which covers a large part. As a result of that, we can actually interconnect and combine a great database about the whole Estonia... this would then enable us to make some kind of a product for attracting interest... (data expert from third sector organisation)

The first example illustrates a situation where open data sharing can have negative consequences for an organisation, particularly in the private sector, due to the potential risk of trade secret leaks. The second example demonstrates a scenario where even governmental statistical organisations and state agencies, which should ideally have the ability to use these data, recognise the significant potential of digital data in creating welfare. However, realising this ideal of welfare is hindered by restrictions on data usage and the integration of large datasets. Nevertheless, it is seen that, similar to the private sector, data are treated as an economic 'product' that can be used to 'sell' the idea of prudent management through data-based approaches to potential stakeholders.

The openness paradox directs our attention to the tensions between two conflicting trends: the push for open government data, data sharing and open data platforms on one hand and the imperative to safeguard data due to concerns related to privacy, security and misuse risks on the other hand (Baack, 2015; Crosas et al., 2015; Check Hayden, 2012; De Filippi & Maurel, 2015; Foege et al., 2019; McBride et al., 2018; Mergel et al., 2018; Robinson, 2020; Robinson & Scassa, 2022; Schrock & Shaffer, 2017; Verhulst & Young, 2015). Despite recent efforts to increase data reuse (Thylstrup et al., 2021), particularly in the context of preventing digital waste and ensuring environmental sustainability, the use of algorithmic approaches across state borders is constrained by location-specific, domain-specific and contextual limitations (Masso, Kaun, & van Noordt, 2023). Consequently, despite the universalist claims associated with data usage, machine learning and automation (Bousquet et al., 2020), the significance of context, location and contextual considerations remains substantial (Kitchin & Dodge, 2011; Loukissas, 2019; Masso et al., 2022; Milan & Treré, 2019). As a result, in this book, we understand the concept of the data welfare state as an ideal type – a model – within the broader framework of social transformations, welfare state regimes and process of automation. Its specific manifestations can significantly vary across different country contexts.

In sum, besides these key developments, mapped in this subsection, there are other interrelated societal transformations happening in the political and economic systems, state-individual relations, interpersonal relationships and people's lifestyles. Alongside these general shifts, there are unique changes in the ideas and practices related to welfare, all of which have created a fertile environment for the emergence and evolution of automated decision-making (ADM) in the welfare sector – a new social order often referred to as 'data welfare'. Nevertheless, the social mechanisms and forces behind these transformations leading to automated welfare remain elusive due to their intricate and interconnected nature, as we have previously discussed. In the following subsection, we aim to identify some of the driving forces that can provide insight into the social shifts towards the emerging reality and structure of the data welfare state.

Unravelling the Forces Behind the Data Welfare State

What are the driving forces behind the data welfare state? What are the societal factors, policy changes and technological innovations that fuel the automation of public services? And what is changing within the data welfare state compared to the welfare state?

Table 1.1 compares the welfare state and the data welfare state, focusing on the underlying normative principles and the driving forces behind both processes.

Based on the mapping of historical developments, this subsection explains the main underlying social mechanisms that have led to and explained the variations in automation across countries, cases and domains and related consequences. Besides the infrastructural and structural shifts explained in the previous sections, there are significant social shifts, like changing social interactions and elaborations. These changing interactions include, for example, shifts in the state–individual relationships (Tammpuu et al., 2022; Tammpuu & Masso, 2019), like increasing risk personalisation and self-enhancement (Perez, 2010), the abstraction of the state (De Kimpe et al., 2022; Terpstra et al., 2022; Verhage et al., 2022) or social exclusion (Park & Humphry, 2019).

Table 1.1 Comparison of the Welfare State and the Data Welfare State

	Welfare state	Data welfare state
Related concepts	Social and economic well-being, welfare, welfare state/institutions, welfare provision, citizens' protection from market risks, welfare services, social justice	Data, datafication, automation, automated decision-making, algorithmic governance, data-based/data-driven/data-informed decision-making
Main underlying principles, related social processes	Equality of opportunities, equitable distribution of wealth, public responsibility	Effective and efficient public services, providing algorithmic infrastructure
Unintended consequences on society, state and individuals	No consensus on the level of state service provision; unfair provision of resources; the ineffectiveness of the state bureaucracies; does not correspond to the needs; and does not provide incentives for productive work. Paternalistic tendencies following discriminatory logics of deviant behaviour and populations	Automating inequalities, datafied discrimination, abstractisation/distanciation of state, loss of jobs due to automation, risks to privacy and transparency, surveillance, overemphasis on welfare growth
Evoking/interrelated economic, political, social and cultural and forces	Social insurance, social rights, social services, government's regulatory, fiscal, monetary and labour market policies	Digitalisation, computational turn, ageing population, welfare state 'crisis', liberal economy, public administration reform, social transformations
Examples across main welfare domains	Unemployment, old age, accidents, sickness, public education, crime prevention, homelessness, social insurance, housing	Predictive policing, healthcare automation, algorithmic education, job seekers' risk classification, social scoring

Source: Authors' table.

On the other hand, several social elaborations and new forms of activism and institutionalisation are emerging, like data activism (Dencik et al., 2016; Grosman & Reigeluth, 2019; Kidd, 2019; Lehtiniemi & Ruckenstein, 2018; Milan & van der Velden, 2016; Van Der Velden, 2015), pioneer communities and hacking communities (Hepp, 2016; Hepp & Loosen, 2019; Männiste & Masso, 2020; Pybus et al., 2015), resistance to automation (Dencik et al., 2016; Ettlinger, 2018; Graham, 2020) or data donation (Skatova & Goulding, 2019). However, in this book, we emphasise the central role of cultural processes in these transformations and driving the automation in public services (see Chapter 3), like the importance of values, including public and social values (Crawford, 2016; Fatima et al., 2020; Inglehart, 1977; Jørgensen & Bozeman, 2007; Prainsack, 2019; Robinson, 2020; Viscusi et al., 2020; Wang, 2022; Wang et al., 2022).

As Table 1.1 indicates, the data welfare state represents a modern adaptation of welfare principles through the integration of data, datafication, automation and algorithmic governance. This evolution focuses on providing effective and efficient public services by leveraging algorithmic infrastructures. The shift towards data-based, data-driven or data-informed decision-making seeks to enhance the responsiveness and precision of welfare provisions. Yet, the transition to a data welfare state also brings about significant unintended consequences. Automating inequalities and datafied discrimination are prominent risks, as algorithmic systems can perpetuate existing biases and injustices. The abstraction and distancing of the state, where decisions are made by algorithms rather than human judgement, can lead to shifting state-citizen relations and pose serious threats to privacy and transparency. Furthermore, the over-emphasis on welfare enhancement through technological means may result in pervasive surveillance and a potential neglect of the human elements of welfare provision.

The emergence of the data welfare state is driven by various interrelated forces. Digitalisation and the computational turn are key technological drivers, while the ageing population and the perceived crisis of the traditional welfare state push for new solutions. The liberal economy, public administration reform and broader social transformations also play significant roles in this evolution. Examples of the data welfare state in action can be seen in predictive policing, healthcare automation, algorithmic education, job seekers' risk classification and social scoring systems. These applications illustrate how data and algorithms are being used to address traditional welfare concerns in new and potentially more efficient ways, although not without introducing new ethical and practical challenges.

In summary, both the welfare state and the data welfare state aim to enhance social well-being, but they operate on different principles and face unique challenges. The welfare state emphasises equitable distribution and public responsibility, while the data welfare state focuses on efficiency and technological integration. Understanding the underlying social mechanisms and drivers of these phenomena is crucial for addressing their respective benefits and pitfalls in the quest for a just and effective social welfare system.

We can generalise that the shift towards a data welfare state is driven by three primary mechanisms. Firstly, digitalisation, encompassing datafication and computation, revolutionises how data are collected, processed and utilised, enabling more precise and efficient welfare services. Secondly, the evolving concept of welfare as a value and practice reflects changing societal norms and expectations about what is considered right and fair. This includes the integration of new values into social norms and practices, influencing individual, societal and state perspectives on welfare. Thirdly, decision-making processes are being transformed by new practices of knowledge construction, which necessitate improved literacy, particularly in public administration. This transformation is further influenced by economic processes such as liberalisation and rapid economic changes, along with crises inherent to the global capitalist order, which drive the need for innovative approaches to managing and delivering welfare.

However, these main mechanisms constitute diverse and highly varied combinations along with the variations in the interrelated transformations in the welfare ideas and institutional settings on the one hand and introducing computational technologies on the other hand. To explore these diverse and complex mechanisms, we need to ground our understanding of the data welfare state empirically. We do this by exploring in-depth case studies of specific implementations across Estonia and Sweden, with some excursions to Germany.

Variations of Welfare Automation and the Data Welfare State

One of the central arguments we make in the book is – context matters! The context of the countries, organisations, institutions and domains where the ADM tools are implemented, but also the temporal context, when these solutions are developed and applied.

The importance of social context is highlighted in numerous prior research. For example, one of the challenges in data science has been developing machine learning models applicable to all types of social contexts. These studies have estimated the particular calculation methods (e.g. classification and regression; see Chowdhury et al., 2023; Yuvalı et al., 2022) or strived to develop and test the new methods such as multimodal developing data models combining text and images (e.g. Hitzler & Sarker, 2022; Kline et al., 2022; Mai et al., 2023), which would provide better opportunities for implementing data models across societies. Also, interdisciplinary critical data studies (e.g. Couldry & Mejias, 2019; Edwards, 2013; Hepp et al., 2022; Iliadis & Russo, 2016; Schäfer & Van Es, 2017) and science and technology studies (e.g. Amoore, 2020; Cristianini et al., 2021; Hagendorff, 2020; Hodapp & Hanelt, 2022; Wimmer et al., 2018) have emphasised the importance of social context in design, testing and use of data. For example, researchers have examined the variations of applying data technologies across various cases, domains and societies (e.g. Bates et al., 2016; Kang, 2023; Yesilbağ, 2022).

However, the applicability of machine learning models in different social contexts is still unresolved. One of the reasons for such a research gap is the lack of knowledge about how to consider the critical social and cultural characteristics of various people and societies in the models' design and development (Acharya et al., 2022; Bansak et al., 2018; Gritsenko et al., 2022; Masso & Kasapoglu, 2020; Milan & Treré, 2019). Recent research (de Bruijn et al., 2022) highlights that shaping common values is critical to ensure the usability of machine learning models in a particular social context at a specific time. However, there are still significant research gaps since we still do not know why the values vary across and within societies, how they spread across areas and how to reduce value conflicts when models are designed and applied in various societies. Besides, prior research has mainly revealed and critically evaluated unintended negative consequences like potential risks and harms related to data transfers, such as reproducing inequalities (Eubanks, 2018), increasing discrimination (Noble, 2018) or constant surveillance (Ferguson, 2017). Besides, most of these studies have been conducted within a single country context. Therefore, in this book, we emphasise the importance of social context (Kitchin & Dodge, 2011; Loukissas, 2019) in the designing and using, mundanisation, experiencing and negotiating automated data solutions.

The methodology that we have developed in our research assumes that these contextual variations are traceable through comparing three countries – Estonia, Germany and Sweden. We assume that the countries differ not only in regard to the state and institutional structures, with a focus on the citizens' relation to these structures and their everyday lifeworld. It means that not only the daily lifeworld of the person themselves is intertwined – their immediate experiences, activities and contacts that make up the world of an individual life, which may or may not result from their status and socio-demographic background. In addition, the social context that must be considered in the case of welfare automation is the intertwining of people's everyday lifeworlds with institutional practices, national norms and values regarding the implementation of these solutions (see Table 1.2).

Conceptually, we understand the social context as a highly intersectional and multilevel category and social process. More in detail, the social context could be understood as a wider location, in terms of both geographical location and also the society and culture where specific technological solutions are developed and implemented. This intersectionality means that different dimensions of location may overlap – for example, geographic location often overlaps with national borders. On the other hand, these

Table 1.2 Comparison of Three Data Welfare Systems

	Estonia	Germany	Sweden
Historical principles and grounds for the welfare state model	Transformation state welfare model	Corporatist–statist welfare state model	Social democratic welfare state model
Traditional organisation of welfare provisions	Liberal characteristics with a strong focus on competition and the free market with conservative aspects of limited redistributive policies	Strong stratification between social classes, shaped by religious values, that has an impact on the distribution of care work	Focus on universal support, equality and a strong component of decommodification of public services
State–citizen relationship	Significant transformations in trust in state institutions during the last decades in relation to building up the state institutions	Relatively lower trust in state institutions, critical attitudes to the state institutions' ability to meet the needs of the citizens they serve	Relatively high trust in state institutions, with a long history and practices of citizens' participation
Individuals' life worlds	Digital practices are routines and highly intertwined with the everyday activities and interactions with the state institutions	Longer traditions in public negotiations and awareness building on privacy and data protection issues	Thanks to digital services and open data, citizens are not only users of services but also active designers
Degree of automated decision-making (ADM) in the welfare sector	High degree in ADM and digitalisation, used as a means for branding the country	Less advanced in the process, but high ambitions for the following years	Relatively high degree in ADM and digitalisation

Source: Authors' table.

diverse dimensions of location can diverge – within one country, there can be several cultural understandings, values and norms regarding how privacy, transparency and efficiency are understood in connection with the implementation of automated solutions. In addition, when we talk about automation in the field of welfare, we must take into account that the provision of welfare services can cover very different social categories and people with social status and fields – education, security, work, income, etc. These categories can form separate areas where automated decisions are applied but are often also closely intertwined – for example, income and education are often, but not always, correlated, which must be considered when providing labour market services. So, in most cases, when we talk about the implementation of automated solutions in the field of well-being, it is also a multilevel phenomenon, meaning that not only immediate experiences, activities and contacts make up the world of an individual life, which may or may not result from their status and socio-demographic background. In addition, the social context that must be considered in the case of welfare automation is the intertwining of people's everyday lifeworlds with institutional practices, national norms and values regarding the implementation of these solutions.

Besides understanding the context as a location, both from geographical and social perspective, we also highlight here the importance of context of temporality. Since these countries that we focus on in this book, but also any other country examples, have gone through diverse social transformations not only during the last decades but also last century. Although the speed and extent of these changes can vary significantly, they are still shifts that need to be considered when we look at the transition to digitalisation and the introduction of automated solutions. We assume that these temporalities and context of time are not only visible in the current practices, ideals and formulations of the welfare state but also exploring the patterns, evolutions and variations of the welfare automation in these countries. In this book and in the following empirical examples, we will illustrate these temporal, spatial and social contextual processes more in detail, with the special focus on the mundanisation, experiences and resistances to automated welfare state (Chapter 2).

Besides these general spatial and temporal variations and patterns of data welfare state, we also argue that the institutional context and the domain-related peculiarities play a crucial role. The institutional context means that different welfare institutions and national institutions may engage with different urge and practices in the implementation of automated solutions. In this book, we argue, based on empirical research, that organisational culture and data activists in institutions play an important role as the initiator and driver of such changes. The Estonian Tax and Customs Board and the Estonian Transport Administration board in the case of Estonia are just a few examples of where either progressive managers of the institution or active data analysts have initiated organisational change and introduced data-based change management practices and ideals in the institution. Although it may be desirable to try to develop universally functioning solutions or to transfer one solution to another field, it is important to take into account the specifics of different domain, as well as the prevailing values and norms, based on which it is desired to offer welfare services and to carry out its automation in the given field (see Chapter 3).

Conclusions

When exploring the emerging data welfare state, we must keep in mind that it is essentially an experimental phenomenon, process and practices. Although depending on the country and the field, automation has been implemented to a different extent. Implementation is often not only happening in the form of the preliminary pilots and experiments, innovation and technological change often happens over a longer period and in subtle ways that are difficult to trace beyond ambitious, performative imaginaries. In this book, we understand the data welfare state and analyse it as a social transformation. Changes can include long-term, decades-long or centuries-long transformations in providing welfare provision and introducing ADM, and medium-term shifts in institutions, such as the transition to a data-based organisational culture. These shifts also involve change processes that are relatively short-term and that are related to the implementation of specific automation projects, such as introducing automation in the field of unemployment. To understand these complex changes, we must simultaneously look at interrelated social and structural processes centred on active human agents who initiate, but also experience or actively resist, these processes of change. In addition, we understand data welfare as a historically embedded process, to understand which, as well as to characterise the variations and specific outputs, we have to look at two intertwined processes – the creation of the welfare state and the history of computing.

Finally, we emphasise the importance of the context in the case of the data welfare state project, which includes the state, society and institutional context, people's everyday characteristics arising from socio-demographic structures and the everyday life world, as well as the intersectional and multi-level interweaving of the two. In the following chapters, these contextualities and intersectionalities will be discussed in more detail, with a special focus on the mundanisation, experiences and resistances of the data welfare state.

References

Abolhassan, F. (2017). *The drivers of digital transformation: Why there's no way around the cloud*. Springer International Publishing.

Acharya, A., Bansak, K., & Hainmueller, J. (2022). Combining outcome-based and preference-based matching: A constrained priority mechanism. *Political Analysis*, *30*(1), 89–112. https://doi.org/10.1017/pan.2020.48

Amoore, L. (2020). *Cloud ethics: Algorithms and the attributes of ourselves and others*. Duke University Press.

Archer, M. S. (1995). *Realist social theory: The morphogenetic approach*. Cambridge University Press.

Archer, M. S. (2010). Routine, reflexivity, and realism *. *Sociological Theory*, *28*(3), 272–303. https://doi.org/10.1111/j.1467-9558.2010.01375.x

Archer, M. S. (2013). *Social morphogenesis* (Vol. 1). Springer.

Archer, M. S., & Maccarini, A. M. (2021). *What is essential to being human?: Can AI robots not share it?* (1st ed.). Routledge.

Baack, S. (2015). Datafication and empowerment: How the open data movement re-articulates notions of democracy, participation, and journalism. *Big Data & Society, 2*(2). https://doi.org/10.1177/2053951715594634

Bansak, K., Ferwerda, J., Hainmueller, J., Dillon, A., Hangartner, D., Lawrence, D., & Weinstein, J. (2018). Improving refugee integration through data-driven algorithmic assignment. *Science, 359*(6373), 325–329. https://doi.org/10.1126/science.aao4408

Bates, J., Lin, Y.-W., & Goodale, P. (2016). Data journeys: Capturing the socio-material constitution of data objects and flows. *Big Data & Society, 3*(2). https://doi.org/10.1177/2053951716654502

Bennett, C. J., & Lyon, D. (2019). Data-driven elections: Implications and challenges for democratic societies. *Internet Policy Review, 8*(4). https://policyreview.info/data-driven-elections

Bodmer, H. (2021). *The other computer history: Amazing, amusing and expierenced stories about the computer science from 1959–2004*. BoD – Books on Demand.

Bousquet, O., Hanneke, S., Moran, S., van Handel, R., & Yehudayoff, A. (2020). A theory of universal learning (arXiv:2011.04483). *arXiv*. https://doi.org/10.48550/arXiv.2011.04483

Braun, J. V., Archer, M. S., Reichberg, G. M., & Sanchez-Sorondo, M. (Eds.). (2021). *Robotics, AI, and humanity: Science, ethics, and policy*. Springer International Publishing. https://doi.org/10.1007/978-3-030-54173-6

Carlson, M. (2018). Automating judgment? Algorithmic judgment, news knowledge, and journalistic professionalism. *New Media & Society, 20*(5), 1755–1772. https://doi.org/10.1177/1461444817706684

Check Hayden, E. (2012). Open-data project aims to ease the way for genomic research. *Nature*. https://doi.org/10.1038/nature.2012.10507

Chowdhury, M. Z. I., Leung, A. A., Walker, R. L., Sikdar, K. C., O'Beirne, M., Quan, H., & Turin, T. C. (2023). A comparison of machine learning algorithms and traditional regression-based statistical modeling for predicting hypertension incidence in a Canadian population. *Scientific Reports, 13*(1), 13. https://doi.org/10.1038/s41598-022-27264-x

Couldry, N., & Mejias, U. (2019). *The costs of connection: How data is colonizing human life and appropriating it for capitalism*. Stanford University Press.

Crawford, K. (2016). Can an algorithm be agonistic? Ten scenes from life in calculated publics. *Science, Technology & Human Values, 41*(1), 77–92. https://doi.org/10.1177/0162243915589635

Cristianini, N., Scantamburlo, T., & Ladyman, J. (2021). The social turn of artificial intelligence. *AI & SOCIETY*. https://doi.org/10.1007/s00146-021-01289-8

Crosas, M., King, G., Honaker, J., & Sweeney, L. (2015). Automating open science for big data. *The ANNALS of the American Academy of Political and Social Science, 659*(1), 260–273.

Dalton, P. S., Ghosal, S., & Mani, A. (2016). Poverty and aspirations failure. *The Economic Journal, 126*(590), 165–188.

de Bruijn, H., Warnier, M., & Janssen, M. (2022). The perils and pitfalls of explainable AI: Strategies for explaining algorithmic decision-making. *Government Information Quarterly*, *39*(2), 101666.

De Filippi, P., & Maurel, L. (2015). The paradoxes of open data and how to get rid of it? Analysing the interplay between open data and sui-generis rights on databases. *International Journal of Law and Information Technology*, *23*(1), 1–22.

De Kimpe, S., Easton, M., & Verhage, A. (2022). Introducing policing in smart cities: Reflections on the abstract police. In A. Verhage, M. Easton, & S. De Kimpe (Eds.), *Policing in smart societies: Reflections on the abstract police* (pp. 1–7). Springer International Publishing. https://doi.org/10.1007/978-3-030-83685-6_1

Dencik, L., Hintz, A., & Cable, J. (2016). Towards data justice? The ambiguity of anti-surveillance resistance in political activism. *Big Data & Society*, *3*(2). https://doi.org/10.1177/2053951716679678

Dencik, L., Hintz, A., Redden, J., & Treré, E. (2019). Exploring data justice: Conceptions, applications and directions. *Information, Communication & Society*, *22*(7), 873–881.

Dencik, L., & Kaun, A. (2020). Datafication and the welfare state. *Global Perspectives*, *1*(1), 12912. https://doi.org/10.1525/gp.2020.12912

Desrosières, A. (1998). *The politics of large numbers: A history of statistical reasoning*. Harvard University Press.

Donati, P. (2021). Impact of AI/robotics on human relations: Co-Evolution through hybridisation. In J. von Braun, M. S. Archer, G. M. Reichberg, M. S. Sorondo (Eds.), *Robotics, AI, and humanity science, ethics, and policy* (pp. 213–227). Springer International Publishing.

Drechsler, W. (2019). Kings and indicators: Options for governing without numbers. In M. J. Prutsch (Ed.), *Science, numbers and politics* (pp. 227–262). Springer International Publishing. https://doi.org/10.1007/978-3-030-11208-0_11

Edwards, P. N. (2013). *A vast machine: Computer models, climate data, and the politics of global warming (illustrated edition)*. The MIT Press.

Egbert, S. (2019). Predictive policing and the platformization of police work. *Surveillance and Society*, *17*(1/2), 83–88. https://doi.org/10.24908/ss.v17i1/2.12920

Engin, Z., & Treleaven, P. (2019). Algorithmic government: Automating public services and supporting civil servants in using data science technologies. *The Computer Journal*, *62*(3), 448–460. https://doi.org/10.1093/comjnl/bxy082

Esping-Andersen, G. (1990). *The three worlds of welfare capitalism*. Princeton University Press.

Ettlinger, N. (2018). Algorithmic affordances for productive resistance. *Big Data & Society*, *5*(1). https://doi.org/10.1177/2053951718771399

Eubanks, V. (2018). *Automating inequality: How high-tech tools profile, police, and punish the poor* (1st ed.). St. Martin's Press.

Fatima, S., Desouza, K. C., & Dawson, G. S. (2020). National strategic artificial intelligence plans: A multi-dimensional analysis. *Economic Analysis and Policy*, *67*(C), 178–194.

Ferguson, A. G. (2017). *The rise of big data policing: Surveillance, race, and the future of law enforcement*. NYU Press.

Foege, J. N., Lauritzen, G. D., Tietze, F., & Salge, T. O. (2019). Reconceptualizing the paradox of openness: How solvers navigate sharing-protecting tensions in crowdsourcing. *Research Policy*, *48*(6), 1323–1339.

Fuchs, C. (2015). *Culture and economy in the age of social media*. Routledge.
Gates, K. (2019). Policing as digital platform. *Surveillance and Society, 17*(1/2), 63–68. https://doi.org/10.24908/ss.v17i1/2.12940
Glasze, G., & Dammann, F. (2021). Von der „globalen Informationsgesellschaft" zum „Schengenraum für Daten" – Raumkonzepte in der Regierung der „digitalen Transformation" in Deutschland. In T. Döbler, C. Pentzold, C. Katzenbach (Hrg.), *Räume digitaler Kommunikation* (pp. 159–182). Halem.
Graham, M. (2020). Regulate, replicate, and resist—The conjunctural geographies of platform urbanism. *Urban Geography, 41*(3), 453–457. https://doi.org/10.1080/02723638.2020.1717028
Gritsenko, D., Markham, A., Pötzsch, H., & Wijermars, M. (2022). Algorithms, contexts, governance: An introduction to the special issue. *New Media & Society, 24*(4), 835–844. https://doi.org/10.1177/14614448221079037
Grosman, J., & Reigeluth, T. (2019). Perspectives on algorithmic normativities: Engineers, objects, activities. *Big Data & Society, 6*(2). https://doi.org/10.1177/2053951719858742
Haardörfer, R. (2019). Taking quantitative data analysis out of the positivist era: Calling for theory-driven data-informed analysis. *Health Education & Behavior, 46*(4), 537–540. https://doi.org/10.1177/1090198119853536
Hagendorff, T. (2020). The ethics of AI Ethics: An evaluation of guidelines. *Minds and Machines, 30*(1), 99–120. https://doi.org/10.1007/s11023-020-09517-8
Halpern, O. (2015). *Beautiful data: A history of vision and reason since 1945*. Duke University Press Books.
Heinrich, S. (2015). Socio-economic consequences of digital transformation. *Socioeconomica: Scientific Journal for Theory and Practice of Socio-economic Development, 3*(6), 176–202. https://doi.org/10.12803/SJSECO.369814
Hepp, A. (2016). Pioneer communities: Collective actors in deep mediatisation. *Media, Culture & Society, 38*(6), 918–933. https://doi.org/10.1177/0163443716664484
Hepp, A., Jarke, J., & Kramp, L. (2022). *New perspectives in critical data studies. The Ambivalences of data power*. Palgrave McMillan. https://link.springer.com/book/10.1007/978-3-030-96180-0
Hepp, A., & Loosen, W. (2019). Pioneer journalism: Conceptualizing the role of pioneer journalists and pioneer communities in the organizational re-figuration of journalism. *Journalism*. https://doi.org/10.1177/1464884919829277
Hitzler, P., & Sarker, M. K. (2022). *Neuro-symbolic artificial intelligence: The state of the art*. Ios Pr Inc.
Hodapp, D., & Hanelt, A. (2022). Interoperability in the era of digital innovation: An information systems research agenda. *Journal of Information Technology*. https://doi.org/10.1177/02683962211064304
Iliadis, A., & Russo, F. (2016). Critical data studies: An introduction. *Big Data & Society, 3*(2). https://doi.org/10.1177/2053951716674238
Inglehart, R. (1977). *The silent revolution: Changing values and political styles among western publics*. Princeton University Press. https://www.jstor.org/stable/j.ctt13x18ck
Jørgensen, T. B., & Bozeman, B. (2007). Public values: An inventory. *Administration & Society, 39*(3), 354–381. https://doi.org/10.1177/0095399707300703

Kang, E. B. (2023). Ground truth tracings (GTT): On the epistemic limits of machine learning. *Big Data & Society*, *10*(1). https://doi.org/10.1177/20539517221146122

Kanger, L. (2016). *Deep transitions: Emergence, acceleration, stabilization and directionality*. SPRU – Science and Technology Policy Research, University of Sussex. http://EconPapers.repec.org/RePEc:sru:ssewps:2016-15

Karatzogianni, A., Nuyen, D., & Serafinelli, E. (2016). *The digital transformation of the public sphere: Conflict, migration, crisis and culture in digital networks*. Palgrave Macmillan.

Karppi, T. (2018). *Disconnect: Facebook's affective bonds*. University of Minnesota Press.

Kaun, A., Larsson, A. O., & Masso, A. (2023). Automating public administration: Citizens' attitudes towards automated decision-making across Estonia, Sweden, and Germany. *Information, Communication & Society*, 1–19. https://doi.org/10.1080/1369118X.2023.2205493

Kempeneer, S., & Heylen, F. (2023). Virtual state, where are you? A literature review, framework and agenda for failed digital transformation. *Big Data & Society*, *10*(1). https://doi.org/10.1177/20539517231160528

Kennedy, H., & Moss, G. (2015). *Known or knowing publics? Social media data mining and the question of public agency*. http://eprints.whiterose.ac.uk/91180/1/2053951715611145.full.pdf

Kidd, D. (2019). Extra-activism: Counter-mapping and data justice. *Information, Communication & Society*, *22*(7), 954–970. https://doi.org/10.1080/1369118X.2019.1581243

Kitchin, R. (2014). Big Data, new epistemologies and paradigm shifts. *Big Data & Society*, *1*(1). https://doi.org/10.1177/2053951714528481

Kitchin, R., & Dodge, M. (2011). *Code/Space: Software and everyday life*. MIT Press.

Kline, A., Wang, H., Li, Y., Dennis, S., Hutch, M., Xu, Z., Wang, F., Cheng, F., & Luo, Y. (2022). Multimodal machine learning in precision health: A scoping review. *Npj Digital Medicine*, *5*(1), Article 1. https://doi.org/10.1038/s41746-022-00712-8

Larsson, K. K., & Haldar, M. (2021). Can computers automate welfare? Norwegian efforts to make welfare policy more effective. *Journal of Extreme Anthropology*, *5*(1), Article 1. https://doi.org/10.5617/jea.8231

Lauristin, M., Masso, A., & Opermann, S. (2017). Introduction: Mapping European social transformations. In *The Routledge international handbook of European social transformations* (pp. 1–19). Routledge.

Lehtiniemi, T., & Ruckenstein, M. (2018). The social imaginaries of data activism. *Big Data & Society*, *6*(1). https://doi.org/10.1177/2053951718821146

Loukissas, Y. A. (2019). *All data are local: Thinking critically in a data-driven society*. MIT Press.

Lowrie, I. (2018). Algorithms and automation: an introduction. *Cultural Anthropology*, *33*(3), 349–359.

Männiste, M., & Masso, A. (2020). 'Three drops of blood for the devil': Data pioneers as intermediaries of algorithmic governance ideals. *Mediální Studia | Media Studies*, *14*(1), 55–74.

Mai, S., Sun, Y., Zeng, Y., & Hu, H. (2023). Excavating multimodal correlation for representation learning. *Information Fusion*, *91*, 542–555. https://doi.org/10.1016/j.inffus.2022.11.003

Masso, A., Chukwu, M., & Calzati, S. (2022). (Non)negotiable spaces of algorithmic governance: Perceptions on the Ubenwa health app as a 'relocated' solution. *New Media & Society, 24*(4), 845–865. https://doi.org/10.1177/14614448221079027

Masso, A., & Kasapoglu, T. (2020). Understanding power positions in a new digital landscape: Perceptions of Syrian refugees and data experts on relocation algorithm. *Information, Communication & Society, 23*(8), 1203–1219. https://doi.org/10.1080/1369118X.2020.1739731

Masso, A., Kaun, A., & van Noordt, C. (2023). *Basic values in artificial intelligence: Comparative factor analysis in Estonia, Germany, and Sweden.* AI & SOCIETY. https://doi.org/10.1007/s00146-023-01750-w

Masso, A., Lauristin, M., Opermann, S., & Kalmus, V. (2020). Applying the morphogenetic perspective for the analysis of Estonian social transformations. In V. Kalmus, M. Lauristin, S. Opermann, T. Vihalemm (Eds.), *Researching Estonian transformation: Morphogenetic reflections* (pp. 1–31). Tartu University Press.

Masso, A., Männiste, M., & Calzati, S. (2023). The social imaginaries on governance through data: Q-methodological analysis of data professionals' views in the field of mobility. *Futures, 152*, 103199. https://doi.org/10.1016/j.futures.2023.103199

Masso, A., Tiidenberg, K., & Siibak, A. (2020a). *How to understand the datafied world? A methodological guide* (SSRN Scholarly Paper ID 4034321). Social Science Research Network. https://papers.ssrn.com/abstract=4034321

Masso, A., Tiidenberg, K., & Siibak, A. (Eds.). (2020b). *Kuidas mõista andmestunud maailma? Metodoloogiline teejuht (How to understand the datafied world? Methodological guide).* TLÜ Kirjastus.

McBride, K., Toots, M., Kalvet, T., & Krimmer, R. (2018). Leader in e-government, laggard in open data: Exploring the case of Estonia. *Revue Française d'administration Publique, 167*(3), 613–625. https://doi.org/10.3917/rfap.167.0613

Mergel, I., Edelmann, N., & Haug, N. (2019). Defining digital transformation: Results from expert interviews. *Government Information Quarterly, 36*(4), 101385. https://doi.org/10.1016/j.giq.2019.06.002

Mergel, I., Gong, Y., & Bertot, J. (2018). Agile government: Systematic literature review and future research. *Government Information Quarterly, 35*(2), 291–298.

Milan, S., & Treré, E. (2019). Big Data from the South(s): Beyond Data Universalism. *Television & New Media, 20*(4), 319–335. https://doi.org/10.1177/1527476419837739

Milan, S., & van der Velden, L. (2016). The Alternative Epistemologies of Data Activism. *Digital Culture & Society, 2*(2), 2364–2114. https://doi.org/10.14361/dcs-2016-0205

Morley, D. (2013). On living in a techno-globalised world: Questions of history and geography. *Telematics and Informatics, 30*(2), 61–65. https://doi.org/10.1016/j.tele.2012.08.001

Noble, S. U. (2018). *Algorithms of oppression: How search engines reinforce racism.* NYU Press.

O'Neil, C. (2016). *Weapons of math destruction: How big data increases inequality and threatens democracy* (1st ed.). Crown.

Oorschot, W. V., Opielka, M., & Pfau-Effinger, B. (Eds.). (2008). *Culture and welfare state: Values and social policy in comparative perspective.* Edward Elgar Publishing.

Pan, J. (2020). *Welfare for autocrats: How social assistance in China cares for its rulers: How social assistance in China cares for its rulers* (1st ed.). Oxford University Press.

Park, S., & Humphry, J. (2019). Exclusion by design: Intersections of social, digital and data exclusion. *Information, Communication & Society, 22*(7), 934–953. https://doi.org/10.1080/1369118X.2019.1606266

Pentland, A. S. (2013). The data-driven society. *Scientific American, 309*(4), 78. https://doi.org/10.1038/scientificamerican1013-78

Perez, C. (2010). Technological revolutions and techno-economic paradigms. *Cambridge Journal of Economics, 34*(1), 185–202. https://doi.org/10.1093/cje/bep051

Poell, T., Nieborg, D., & Van Dijck, J. (2019). Platformisation. *Internet Policy Review, 8*(4), 1–13.

Prainsack, B. (2019). Logged out: Ownership, exclusion and public value in the digital data and information commons. *Big Data & Society, 6*(1). https://doi.org/10.1177/2053951719829773

Pybus, J., Coté, M., & Blanke, T. (2015). Hacking the social life of Big Data. *Big Data & Society, 2*(2). https://doi.org/10.1177/2053951715616649

Robinson, S. C. (2020). Trust, transparency, and openness: How inclusion of cultural values shapes Nordic national public policy strategies for artificial intelligence (AI). *Technology in Society, 63*, 101421. https://doi.org/10.1016/j.techsoc.2020.101421

Robinson, P., & Scassa, T. (2022). *The future of open data*. University of Ottawa Press/Les Presses de l'Universite d'Ottawa.

Süssenguth, F. (2015). *Die Gesellschaft der Daten: Über die digitale Transformation der sozialen Ordnung*. Transcript Verlag.

Schäfer, M. T., & Van Es, K. (2017). *The datafied society: Studying culture through data*. Amsterdam University Press.

Schlüter, E., Masso, A., & Davidov, E. (2019). What factors explain anti-Muslim prejudice? A comparative assessment of Muslim population size, institutional characteristics and immigration-related media claims. *Journal of Ethnic and Migration Studies*, 1–16.

Schrock, A., & Shaffer, G. (2017). Data ideologies of an interested public: A study of grassroots open government data intermediaries. *Big Data & Society, 4*(1). https://doi.org/10.1177/2053951717690750

Skatova, A., & Goulding, J. (2019). Psychology of personal data donation. *PLoS One, 14*(11), e0224240. https://doi.org/10.1371/journal.pone.0224240

Tammpuu, P., & Masso, A. (2019). Transnational digital identity as an instrument for global digital citizenship: The case of Estonia's E-residency. *Information Systems Frontiers, 21*(3), 621–634. https://doi.org/10.1007/s10796-019-09908-y

Tammpuu, P., Masso, A., Ibrahimi, M., & Abaku, T. (2022). Estonian e-residency and conceptions of platform-based state-individual relationship. Trames. *Journal of the Humanities and Social Sciences, 26*(1), 3. https://doi.org/10.3176/tr.2022.1.01

Taylor, L. (2017). What is data justice? The case for connecting digital rights and freedoms globally. *Big Data & Society, 4*(2). https://doi.org/10.1177/2053951717736335

Terpstra, J., Salet, R., & Fyfe, N. (Eds.). (2022). *The Abstract Police: Critical reflections on contemporary change in police organisations*. Eleven International Publishing.

Thylstrup, N. B., Agostinho, D., Ring, A., D'Ignazio, C., & Veel, K. (2021). *Uncertain archives: Critical keywords for big data*. MIT Press.

Van Der Velden, L. (2015). Forensic devices for activism: Metadata tracking and public proof. *Big Data & Society, 2*(2). https://doi.org/10.1177/2053951715612823

Van Dijck, J., Poell, T., & De Waal, M. (2018). *The platform society: Public values in a connective world*. Oxford University Press.

Verhage, A., Easton, M., & Kimpe, S. D. (2022). *Policing in smart societies: Reflections on the abstract police*. Springer Nature.

Verhulst, S. G., & Young, A. (2015). *Open Data. A twenty-first-century asset for small and médium-sized enterprises*. Recuperado de: https://www.thegovlab.org/static/files/publications/OpenData-and-SME-Final-Aug2015.pdf

Vihalemm, P., Masso, A., & Opermann, S. (2017). *The Routledge international handbook of European social transformations*. Routledge.

Viscusi, G., Rusu, A., & Florin, M.-V. (2020). Public strategies for artificial intelligence: Which value drivers? *Computer, 53*(10), 38–46. https://doi.org/10.1109/MC.2020.2995517

Wang, B. (2022). *Public value and social development*. Springer Nature.

Wang, B., Xia, L., & Wu, A. M. (2022). Social development with public value: An international comparison. *Social Indicators Research, 162*(2), 909–934. https://doi.org/10.1007/s11205-021-02805-5

Wimmer, M. A., Boneva, R., & Ciacomo, D. (2018). Interoperability governance: A Definition and Insights from Case Studies in Europe. In *Proceedings of the 19th Annual International Conference on Digital Government Research Governance in the Data Age - Dgo'. Vol. 18*, pp. 1–11, 1–12. https://dl.acm.org/doi/10.1145/3209281.3209306

Yesilbağ, M. (2022). New geographies of platform capitalism: The case of digital monopolization in Turkey. *Big Data & Society, 9*(2). https://doi.org/10.1177/20539517221124585

Yuvalı, M., Yaman, B., & Tosun, Ö. (2022). Classification comparison of machine learning algorithms using two independent CAD datasets. *Mathematics, 10*(3), Article 3. https://doi.org/10.3390/math10030311

2
The Mundanisation of Algorithmic Public Services

Scene: Jüri's visit to the Unemployment Office. I, Jüri, reside in South Estonia amidst the forests, near Valga. The familiar whispers of the woodland fell silent for me when I suddenly found myself without a job. The once flourishing forestry industry now confronted uncertain times, leaving me at the crossroads of insecurity. In search of a lifeline, I stepped into the Estonian Unemployment Insurance Fund office. There, OTT, the digital guide, became my beacon. It analysed my skills and prospects, acknowledging the challenges of the forestry sector's downturn. OTT together with an unemployment fund case worker, offered a tailored plan, suggesting courses for retraining. With a mix of hope and trepidation, I embraced the opportunity. Guided by OTT and unemployment fund case worker, I enroled in courses aligned with the evolving industries in Valga. Still unsure what the future might bring, I tried to remain hopeful putting my trust in the institution and it enhanced possibilities for finding a new line of work for me.

In this chapter, we follow the implementation of data-based public administration through several case studies, including the automation of benefit applications and artificial intelligence (AI) applications developed by the Employment Services. The focus is on mundane practices of sense-making by both civil servants and citizens in the process of implementing data-based automation, a process that we – following Robert Willim (2017) – call mundanisation. We explore how they relate to digital technologies for automation that they are interfacing with in everyday work life. These sense-making practices include, for example, giving algorithms and tools for robotic process automation (RPA) human names as well as treating them as staff within the organisation. This perspective allows us to draw a picture of how new technology is integrated into everyday work lives and hence made mundane until it appears into the background and becomes invisible. This chapter engages with the question how non-technical experts relate to complex systems in their daily work developing mundane strategies of sense-making. This also includes shifts in the profession of caseworkers and civil servants in the welfare sector and their changing tasks as well as self-perceptions.

Mundanisation

The implementation of new technologies in different contexts has triggered extensive engagement, for example, considering the shifts in power relations, de- and reskilling, as well as structural changes in organisational culture. In this chapter, we zoom in on the introduction of data tools for welfare automation through the lens of meaning-making. The meaning-making around technology is related to not only how we imagine technology to work with and for us but also which aspects we ignore to develop mundane, workable understandings of complex systems (Bowker & Leigh Star, 1999; Gitelman, 2008; Peters, 2015). Robert Willim (2017) has defined this process of meaning-making around technology as mundanisation. With reference to domestication theory (Morley & Silverstone, 1990; Silverstone, 2005) that has conceptualised the integration of new technologies in our everyday lives – the taming of new media – he argues that in order to be able to establish mundane uses of technologies, we have to forget and ignore aspects of these systems. Willim argues that mundanisation as a process transmutes technologies that are entangled with our everyday lives. Technologies are made ordinary, mundane and commonplaces. Part of this process are not only lay theories of how technology works but also struggles about defining what technology as such is and does. The definition of what a specific technology is and does in turn has implications on how technology is integrated in, for example, legal frameworks and institutional structures. At the same time, successful technologies are often considered as hidden or invisible infrastructures that slip from our consciousness (Star & Ruhleder, 1996; Willim, 2019).

The process of mundanisation, hence, relates in an almost paradoxical manner to sociotechnical imaginaries of technologies that are often incorporating elements of the sublime and magical thinking. Sociotechnical imaginaries are in many ways aspirational of an impossible future and hence could be seen as standing in contrast with mundane sense-making of technology. Following Willim (2017, 2019), we understand mundanisation as encompassing a dialectic movement between the ordinary and extraordinary, the mundane and the sublime. Struggles around the meaning-making around technologies that are expressed through conflicting definitions and access renders technology that is going through the process of mundanisation visible. Mundanisation as a process involves different forms of meaning-making that include practices of highlighting and forgetting specific technological aspects.

Besides that, a focus on mundanisation allows to re-centre people in the process of automating welfare and the data welfare state going beyond the currently still dominant approaches of *Ethics in AI* discussions. Instead, the engagement with people's everyday life worlds and meaning-making around technology is centred upon (Neyland, 2019; Pink et al., 2022). Let us start to disentangle the process of mundanisation with illustrations from both Sweden and Estonia of not only how the meaning around automated decision-making (ADM) tools is negotiated and part of a broader digitalisation discourse but also how these technical systems become mundane in the everyday work context.

The process of mundanisation emerges in among other things practices of care that are balancing frictions and failures of automation projects. As we will show in the following specific actors take caring roles sometimes in the form of digital ambassadors that promote digitalisation and automation projects within the organisation and towards street-level bureaucrats. Other forms of care are related to the preparational tasks including the care of necessary data. As we have discussed in Chapter 1, digital frictions often emerge in the implementation process. Care practices balance these frictions but are also developed in relation to failing data infrastructures once a new system is implemented. Accordingly, we trace the mundanisation process across care practices, frictions and failure.

From Rebel to Model: Automating Benefit Applications

In Sweden, the aim to achieve high levels of digitalisation has been strong for a long time and can be traced back in earlier government enquiries, commissions and strategy documents. One of the largest investments in computerisation and extension digitalisation began in the late 1970s with the data delegation spanning several years and providing numerous reports as well as practical work programmes to increase skills and literacy levels of the general public about computers in connection with the computerisation of public administration. More recently, there are a number of strategic government initiatives that are focused on digitalisation and lately AI including the national strategy for digitalisation and the formation of the national AI commission. Here, the public sector has been identified as one important domain that could draw huge advantages from enhanced digitalisation. The general digitalisation policies are supposed to push Sweden to become the 'best' in digitalisation in the world (Regeringen, n.d.). In the 2017 digitalisation strategy, this not-very-modest aim was specified and linked to sustainability goals as well. The recent government has announced in late 2023 the formation of a new AI commission to push AI developments in Sweden and support innovation that puts the country on the AI map globally. The commission will also support the government in developing a new digital and AI-related strategy, updating the one published in 2017 (Regeringen, 2023).

These strategic developments need to be translated into not only specific programmes but also legal frameworks that, for example, regulate the use of ADM and AI in the public sector. Until recently, different legal frameworks were partly contradicting each other. Therefore in 2018, the legal framework for municipalities (Kommunallagen) was updated to allow for ADM on the municipal level (Sveriges Kommuner och Regioner).

While these are important contextual developments, we are here more interested in how technology is made sense of in the actual operations of the public sector, that is, how they are made mundane. One, by now, historical example to illustrate such sense-making and negotiation processes is the Trelleborg model. Since 2017, the Trelleborg municipality, with a population of approximately 46,000 residents, has implemented a fully ADM system for social benefit applications. This particular case of ADM is widely recognised and frequently discussed in Sweden and beyond. Trelleborg municipality takes pride in its role as a pioneering force in automation, leading the Rebel to Model innovation programme (Rakar, 2018). It serves as a significant reference point for exploring both algorithmic culture and the consequences of the digital welfare state (Choroszewicz & Mäihäniemi, 2020; Kaun, 2022).

The system itself relies on a relatively simple decision tree model that cross-references specific variables with databases, including data from the tax agency, such as income or state health insurance payments. Initially, all applications undergo manual processing by caseworkers. However, subsequent monthly follow-up applications are automatically processed. The individuals affected by this ADM system are residents of the municipality who are seeking economic support, which includes welfare benefits. These benefits can cover various expenses like housing, food, clothing, telephone and internet access.

One of the most debated aspects of implementing this ADM system was the reduction in the number of civil servants handling social benefit applications, dropping from eleven to just three caseworkers. During the year of the algorithm's introduction in 2017, the number of residents no longer dependent on social benefits increased to 450, a significant rise compared to 168 residents five years earlier. It is worth noting that this decline in beneficiaries cannot be solely attributed to the municipality's automation efforts, according to both municipal authorities and journalists. It is also a result of a comprehensive programme aimed at reintegrating long-term unemployed individuals into the job market (Sveriges Television, 2018).

The Trelleborg case has sparked controversy since its early stages. Criticisms have ranged from concerns about the potentially illegal delegation of decision-making to algorithmic systems, which lack proper legal frameworks for municipalities, to questions about transparency and the future role and status of civil servants in general. The Trelleborg municipality defines ADM as 'the automated handling of applications and views rule-based algorithms as decision support systems, rather than autonomous robots to which tasks are entirely delegated' (based on the interview conducted with the project leader of Trelleborg municipality, conducted on 17 October 2018). Even when algorithms generate decisions, each case is overseen by an assigned civil servant who holds formal accountability for all decisions made, as asserted by the project leader at Trelleborg municipality. An interviewee further emphasises that determinations related to social benefits hinge on the applicant's readiness for the job market. The comprehensive evaluation of this criterion remains the responsibility of civil servants and is not delegated to algorithms. In this regard, the municipality advocates for a broad definition of decision support systems that encompasses fully automated sub-decisions but places ultimate responsibility on the designated civil servant. The project leader contends that:

> So, what is automated decision-making actually? This is the question. In our process, when we refer to social benefits, this is mainly a question whether you are available for the job market or not. And the evaluation of this question, this

decision, if you are available or not is taken in the job market process by a civil servant. And then this decision is taken to a higher organizational level and becomes part of the decision by the public agency. So, in that sense, we do not have fully automated decisions. (Interview with project leader Trelleborg municipality).

This understanding and definition mirror legal concerns surrounding accountability and responsibility regarding decisions made with algorithmic assistance, specifically addressing who bears responsibility for the resulting decisions. While the project leader contends that only sub-decisions are automated and that the ultimate responsibility lies with the caseworker for the overall decision, the challenge of explainability persists. When intricate algorithmic systems handle sub-decisions, it can impact the overall decision and potentially render it inadequately explainable.

However, the interviews also revealed a more commonplace form of definitional work. In the mainstream media, the algorithm initially deployed in Trelleborg was dubbed 'Ernst'. The civil servant we have interviewed recollects that:

Ernst, no we do not call it like that anymore. That was a working name that we had, kind of. Just for us to better understand "what is this actually"? And to a certain degree it was some kind of robot, but actually an algorithm. But to make the whole thing a little bit more lively, so when I worked with a working group on this and we had a brain storming day where we were supposed to discuss what we are going to do we kind of... in order to be able to relate to something, and it is kind of difficult to relate to an algorithm, we came up with this exercise. Like a collective drawing exercise of the algorithm on a big flip chart paper, kind of. One person drew one part and then the next person drew another. In that way, we kind of developed a picture. And were like, so this is what you look like and he kind of was born then. And then it was our former head of administration who came up with that he should be called Ernst. But this is nothing we are still using. This was kind of in the beginning of everything (Interview with civil servant Trelleborg municipality).

As highlighted in the quote, during the implementation phase, it was crucial to cultivate a down-to-earth rapport with the impending algorithm. This was accomplished by portraying the system in the guise of a person rather than a procedural flowchart, complemented by assigning it a name. Nonetheless, as the project leader notes, this strategy gradually waned with time, making way for a more formal, technical comprehension:

Yes. I think we have taught ourselves that we should speak of automated handling, but in the beginning, it was that we said, 'it is a robot' and the thing with the name. And sometimes we can still speak of producing a report with help of the robot, but actually we are talking about automation. There is no R2D2 who walks around the corridor, but it is a computer as such. But often it is, maybe it is easier to understand if you call it a handling robot or something like that (Interview with project leader Trelleborg municipality).

A tension exists between the use of technically precise terminology and a more accessible, everyday understanding that enables individuals to relate to a complex technical infrastructure in a familiar manner. While civil servants and unit managers at the municipality are expected to employ terms like 'automation' or 'automated record processing', colloquial language often takes precedence. This was evident in emails sent during the interview from staff at Trelleborg municipality, which included the following image (Figure 2.1), underscoring the perception of the automation process resembling a robot.

In the email signature image, which states, 'When robots take care of the processing, the municipality takes care of the citizens', citizens are portrayed as the beneficiaries of automation. However, in the actual automation process, their involvement is minimal. Both the project leader and the civil servant we interviewed argued that little had fundamentally changed for the citizens. They still receive the same level of service and have identical access to the e-service platform. In many cases, they are unaware that the municipality has automated parts of the application processing in the backend, except for the fact that they receive decisions more rapidly, which aligns with their own interests, as per the interviewees. Hence, the understanding is that better care by the caseworkers is provided since time is saved from administrative tasks. Instead of

När robotar sköter handläggningen
ägnar sig kommunen
åt medborgarna

Figure 2.1 Email Signature Image, Trelleborg Municipality, 2019. 'When Robots Take Care of the Processing, the Municipality Takes Care of the Citizens'
Source: Email signature Trelleborg municipality.

handling paperwork, the caseworkers can now dedicate their time to more intense contacts with clients and attempt to match them with potential employers.

A website instructing residents on how to apply for social benefits mentions the use of RPA for tasks that machines can handle more efficiently, quicker and more reliably than humans. It is also asserted that 'the robot' executes all tasks in the same manner as a caseworker (Trelleborg municipality, 2020). Citizens were not actively involved in the development process, whereas civil servants were extensively engaged as our interviewees indicated. They were filmed, were interviewed and participated in workshops before the coding and implementation stages, with the aim of fostering a sense of participation in the development process, as emphasised by the project leader during the interview. The civil servant acknowledges this and takes pride in 'being an active part of this technological development and being the first in Sweden to do so, staying at the forefront' (Interview with civil servant from Trelleborg municipality.

However, as national and international discussions regarding the role of algorithms in everyday life grew (Neyland, 2019; Ruckenstein, 2023), journalistic investigations and oversight efforts regarding automation in the public sector began to emerge. Both journalists and professional unions affected by cognitive automation projects like the one in Trelleborg became proactive advocates for redefining ADM and making the involved algorithms accessible to the public as public records. Two significant legal cases related to the Trelleborg automation project emerged. In both cases, the definition of the algorithm and ADM varied slightly, highlighting the contentious nature of the process of making automation more familiar through definition.

Automating the Swedish Public Employment Services

Another area that has been increasingly automated is different aspects of the Public Employment Services in Sweden. Meeting considerable cuts with technology, the agency has for a long time been testing different forms of automation of backend record handling. Tracing the implementation of a job seeker profiling tool and an ADM solution for record processing, we zoom in on aspects of care and phatic labour, such as customer service interactions, that are part of the mundanisation process. The Swedish Public Employment Services have in recent years been going through a major organisational transformation that included collaboration with and outsourcing of certain services to private actors to reach more efficiency and reduce the number of caseworkers. Part of this organisational transformation is the increased introduction of data-based, algorithmic automation. As an example of one major project of automation efforts at the employment services serves here the pre-assessment of long-term job seekers that are considered for the programme Rusta och Matcha (train and match) (Arbetsförmedling, 2021a). Based on an initial assessment of job seekers who have been unemployed for at least six months, a suggestion for a private coaching company for training is made. The assessment tool is described as AI based on some 30 variables that consider both individual characteristics of the job seeker such as age, gender, country of birth, place of residence and educational level and statistical, contextual information such as level of unemployment at the place of residency, average income at the place of residency, citizenship spread at the place of residency and share of single households at the place of residency (see Figure 2.2).

Based on the variables, job seekers are profiled and sorted into three categories that distinguish between different probabilities of re-entry into the job market (see Figure 2.2): too close to the job market (no additional training will be proposed), suggestion to participate in one of the three 'train and match' programme groups or too far away from the job market. If the job seekers end up in the train and match category, they are sorted again into three groups that determine which kind of programmes and coaching companies will be offered to the job seeker. The pre-assessment is motivated with higher efficiency and accuracy than manual processing and assessment by caseworkers, namely around 62%, while the accuracy of the caseworkers decisions is calculated with 50% (Carlsson, 2023). An updated model that is based on the same variables and data was introduced in spring 2023. In comparison to the previous model, the new one also considers the length of being registered as a job seeker with the employment services and the actual result of training support. Hence, the new model is more flexible, and the result might vary over time. The accuracy is also considered higher compared to the previous model (Arbetsförmedling, 2021b).

Criteria for evaluating job chances

- Country of birth
- Region
- Zip code
- Town
- Municipality
- Educational level
- Educational focus
- Professions applied for (up to four)
- Age
- Sex
- Member of unemployment insurance
- Month of registration
- Number of days unemployed during the previous registration period

- Number of days since the last registration
- Number of earlier registrations
- Number of days of training during the previous registration period
- Kinds of programs that one participated in during the previous registration period
- Disabilities
- Other characteristics that are used to evaluate the job chances

Data from the statistical office

- Unemployment rate in the living area
- Average income in the living area
- Educational level in the living area
- Citizenship distribution in the living area
- Share of single household in the living area

Figure 2.2 Variables That Calculate the Job Chances of Registered Job Seekers
Source: By the authors based on Swedish Employment Services.

Frictions

The 'train and match' employment tool was initially tested in a pilot with specific municipalities and later rolled out more broadly. The implementation was met with strong criticism by both caseworkers and job seekers, namely that the accuracy was not much higher than pure chance and suggests the wrong training programmes for the job seekers (Lindberg, 2021). At the same time, the head of the AI unit at the Employment Services argued for less involvement of caseworkers as they increase the failure margins (Lindberg, 2021). It was also argued that caseworkers had been making more gender-based decisions discriminating against female job seekers in comparison to the automated tool (Figure 2.3).

According to a study conducted by Vanja Carlsson, the efficiency and equality argument are paramount in legitimising the implementation of the AI tool, not accuracy. During one of her interviews, an interviewee joked that the tool is very just since all job seekers receive equally bad decisions (Carlsson, 2023). Although the profiling tool is presented as a decision support system rather than a fully automated process, the caseworkers have very little room to reconsider decisions made by the tool. Carlsson summarises:

> If the ADM tool says "NO" to support activities, there are no formal alternatives to following that decision. If the tool says "YES," there are nine stated and predetermined reasons for deviating from the decision. These apply in cases where the jobseeker will clearly not be able to participate in training activities—for example, if the jobseeker is pregnant, knows that they will be starting education in the near future, or has certain disabilities (IFAU, 2021, p. 7). (Cited by 2023)

Even in the case that the job seeker is assigned support activities, deviation from the decision is limited. This case of data-based automation illustrates frictions within one public agency that emerge in the context of technological change. During the implementation of emergent technologies, these frictions appear between different groups, here caseworkers and AI developers who are implicated in the implementation process differently. Caseworkers emphasise, as we will also see later, the embodied knowledge and expertise that come with training and experience on the job, while developers focus

Distance from the job market

Other support/ Service	Adjust and evaluate adequacy of the service for the job seeker			Digital support/ service
Too far	C	B	A	Too close

Figure 2.3 Visualisation of the Implications of the Job Chance Calculation
Source: By the authors based on Swedish Employment Services.

on the efficiency and fairness of automated decisions. For both groups, automation also comes with different future expectations. Caseworkers are to a certain extent considered obsolete and even harmful to the decision-making process, while AI-based technologies promise a smooth and cost-efficient future for public agencies. The different positionings have consequences for the implementation and adaptation process including the active resistance by caseworkers.

Failure

In 2019, the Swedish public service broadcaster reported that the Employment Services potentially had issued tens of thousands false decisions with an impact on unemployed receiving benefits (SVT, 2019). This is a typical case of backend automation that is not directly experienced by the citizens but that has potentially direct implications for them, namely warnings and in the worst case payment cancellations. The failure within an automated backend system emerged in connection with registering incoming activity reports that document application and training activities and that have to be submitted monthly by the job seekers. The automated handling of the incoming reports is based on two parameters, namely the eligibility for benefits and that a report is submitted. In case a person is eligible according to the system but has not submitted a report, a warning will be automatically triggered and sent out. As of 2020, there are around 150,000 job seekers who need to submit activity reports every month and among them there are around 11,000 who receive a warning for not submitting the report on time. The most serious sanction for not submitting the report on time is the cancelation of benefit payments for up to 45 days, while the amount is reduced to the minimum level of around 20 EUR per day. Missing the deadline to submit the activity report triggers the automated system to issue first a warning and second the cancelation of benefit payments. The system produces a high volume of interactions, or what the agency calls communications (interview a manager at the Employment Services), with up to 15,000 communications and up to 11,000 automated decisions per month.

This high volume of automatically triggered interactions emerged as a problem when the system failure was discovered. The failure itself was discovered by a civil servant who started to document false warnings or cases in which no decision was taken at all. This led to an investigation with a larger sample of 100–300 cases that was drawn monthly and checked manually. In order to prevent further false decisions and warnings to be sent, the agency went back to manually processing incoming activity reports between October 2018 and May 2019 that was hard to do as the number of caseworkers was reduced previously dramatically. The aim was to understand how the failure happened, what exactly went wrong and at the same time identify all the cases in which a false decision had been issued. After having shifted to manual processing incoming activity reports, a commission was put in place to investigate the failure in depth and the supervisory authority IAF – Inspektionen för arbetslöshetsförsäkringen – investigated the decision-making process as well. In a report published in 2021, IAF reached the conclusion that more sanctions would be issued if the activity reports were processed automatically based on samples that have been analysed more closely (IAF, 2021). At the same time, they also come to the conclusion that specific needs of job seekers would be easier and earlier identified in case of manual processing. In that sense, automation has led to more efficiency and not necessarily harsher sanctions and control of job seekers but the care and support by the agency has decreased as well.

The evaluation of eligibility for unemployment insurance payment requires a certain amount of data. When we conducted our interviews in 2020, there were twelve different parameters that regulate whether a payment is made or withheld. Most of them need an evaluation by a caseworker, and if there are too many parameters involved, automation is difficult. The registration and handling of obligatory reporting on job search activities or the participation in educational training was quickly identified as an area that could be automated. The first project to automate the handling of the so-called activity reports was already implemented in 2014/15 when the *Förvaltningslagen* (law regulating public administration) was still not updated and did not regulate fully automated decisions. The employment services interpreted this as a legal grey zone and started experimenting. One argument that was debunked quickly was efficiency gains. While certain internal practices were eliminated, the calls with questions concerning the correct reporting from citizens increased significantly. In that sense, there was initially not more efficiency, but costs, efforts and related work moved elsewhere instead.

While interviewing caseworkers at different local branches of the employment services, we encounter both enthusiasm for automation projects and concerns:

> Administration, yes... Exactly, that's what I'm saying, that automated administration is great, that it comes in. So, the amount of paperwork to be handled is great. But as I said, when it comes to people, that is, we need to map out what they need, decision-making. That's still where we need to come in. And that's how Försäkringskassan works too. The Social Insurance Agency has this main developed IT system. The computers still don't make decisions. Because if you look at, they have a rehab chain. Their regulations are very square. After you have passed 90 days, then your ability to work should be assessed this against this. And then once you have passed 180 days, you ... your ability to work must be assessed against open work ... And then there are special reasons and so on. This can be entered into computers. And then the computers can ... But they don't choose to do that because they are human beings. The computers are ... well, they will do the work they are told to do, what they are programed to do. However, if I look at a medical certificate. I've worked at the Social Insurance Agency before, so I know if a person has low blood pressure, so for me, it doesn't ... if I don't have medical knowledge, it doesn't give me any signals. Okay, but it's low blood pressure. But the medical advisors there, they said "this can be very dangerous". You know what I mean? So we still need knowledge. As humans, we need to have some knowledge, and you can't input that. A computer can't check every single thing. So it's still ... (civil servant A at local branch 1)

One crucial step in the work of frontline workers at the employment services is the registration process of clients who recently got unemployed. In the interviews, there is a constant back-and-forth arguing for the elimination of boring and repetitive tasks that are strongly regulated for the agency including the registration of new clients and their job market evaluation. Basically the same questionnaire has to be filled by all new clients. Instead of having this done by a caseworker, the evaluation should be automated, some argued. However, at the same time, caseworkers reflected on embodied and practical knowledge that is activated during the evaluation process. This, all were convinced, could hardly be automated.

The relationship to automation from the perspective of those involved in the implementation process is hence ambiguous. Even if the specific person is a tech enthusiast and even takes the role as a digital ambassador, there are always also concerns involved. Embodied knowledge and acquired expertise that is valued. The negotiation of these emerging ambiguities is part of the mundanisation process until they are no longer noticed or an inconvenience.

> And I don't think that decision-making should be left to automation. We still have to apply all the regulations and so on. And it's just like ... if we let the technicians make decisions, then it's exactly the same dilemma as with these self-driving cars. If it causes someone else's collision, who is responsible? So all these government decisions can harm someone else. And then the authority itself should take ... be responsible for the damages, or how about that. And if a computer has made several wrong decisions, and several have caused damage, how many millions will we have to pay, you know? So it's still a human view we need in the decision-making part. But the administrative part, the machines can come and prepare everything and so on, so we can look and ... So I think that part. But I don't think it should take over the decision-making part (civil servant A at local branch 1).

Care

Several caseworkers we spoke with have taken the role as digital coaches at their units. Due to taking this position, they were probably more prone to being selected by their managers for the interviews with us and more likely to agree on meeting us. Their role as digital coaches is encouraged centrally but emerges within the local structures of their specific branch or branches if they rotate to other offices. Their main role is to foster a positive attitude towards datafication of the agency more generally through providing guidance and filtering of information as described:

> I'm a digital coach in our unit, so I'm both here and in the other group. But I haven't worked with [...] yet, the plan is that after the New Year I'll start hanging out there a bit too, supporting them. But yes, so you get a lot of

information here. And it's those who work on digital engagement, I think they're called, who work with the introduction of our various system (civil servant A at local branch 1).

Another caseworker describes the frustration of many colleagues having to work with a plethora of different and most importantly often changing systems. Shifting between different platforms and learning their way through new systems was identified as one of the major sources of frustration as this caseworker argued. Frustration is one of the typical emotions emerging in the context of new digital systems that caseworkers have to interact with needs levelling. Here the digital coaches and ambassadors play important roles and engage with what Kaun and Forsman (2024) have earlier called digital care work.

The concept of digital care work encompasses a category of digital tasks that do not demand specific technical training or skill sets, distinguishing it from other forms of digital work such as digitising text batches, database maintenance or software programming. Digital care work focuses on not only assisting individuals with everyday tasks and activities but also promoting generally positive attitudes towards digital systems in the work context. Tronto (1993) has posited that care involves reaching out to entities beyond oneself, involving 'everything that we do to maintain, continue, and repair our world so that we can live in it as well as possible' (Tronto & Fisher, 1990, p. 40). Care represents a concern of active humans engaged in everyday life, embodying both a practice and a disposition. Notably, the concept of care has gained increased attention in science and technology studies since the early 2010s, with significant works including the edited volume *Care in Practice: On Tinkering in Clinics, Homes and Farms* (Mol et al., 2010) and Puig de la Bellacasa's article (2010) *Matters of care in technoscience: Assembling neglected things*. These works underscore the role of care in technology and, conversely, the role of technology in care. Earlier discussions of care work primarily centred on caregiving within human relationships, such as the mother–child dynamic, often overlooked as invisible domestic labour.

In many respects, the type of work encountered in discussions with caseworkers at the Public Employment Services reminds us of what Kalm (2019) described as academic domestic work in her text 'On academic domestic work and its distribution'. Kalm argues that academic domestic work comprises tasks that are essential for the institution but not assigned to everyone, lacking recognition as meritorious work. This type of work functions as a public good benefiting everyone, making the institution run smoothly while creating a favourable atmosphere. Hence, it can be seen as a public good (Kalm, 2019, p. 11).

Additionally, digital care work can be related to digital labour. Under the notion of the 'digital housewife', Jarrett (2016) encapsulates forms of uncompensated digital labour critical to digital technologies, sharing similarities with domestic labour as it sustains and renews labouring bodies and subjects. This labour, although unpaid or significantly under-compensated, plays a crucial role in maintaining capitalist modes of production. It includes activities like liking and sharing content and conforming to the rules of social media, described by Arcy (2016) as micro-acts of emotional work online. Unlike digital domestic labour (i.e. unpaid and voluntary user activities explored by Jarrett), digital care work performed by care workers is compensated. However, it often goes unrecognised and is not reflected in official statistics.

More generally, the digital care work conducted by caseworkers, beyond the official tasks of processing records and making decisions based on defined rules, takes the shape of what Julia Elyachar (2010) has termed phatic labour. Elyachar develops the concept of phatic labour based on Bronislaw Malinowski's concept of phatic communion, which grabbles with the role of gossip and chatting as a way to establish social ties while not being primarily focused on information exchange. Phatic labour then, Elyachar argues, 'produces communicative channels that can potentially transmit not only language but also all kinds of semiotic meaning and economic value' (2010, p. 453). These established communicative channels act as social infrastructure allowing for in Elyachar's case economic practices and profit generation. The notion of phatic labour has been elaborated on by Singh (2024) considering digital welfare provision in India. Specific key persons emerged there as intermediaries to allow for the participation in digital infrastructures of the state, namely the population registries such as Aadhaar that collects biometric data of Indian citizens across the whole country since 2009. These intermediaries provide hardware infrastructure such as scanners and computers as well as subtle knowledge on which offices are less frequented. Their phatic labour constitutes social aspects of the digital infrastructure. Similarly, caseworkers at the Employment Service consider themselves as intermediaries who translate between administrative, bureaucratic rules and citizens' life worlds. They explain processes and chains of decision-making while making decisions on cases themselves. The so-called governance renewal journey explored in the case of the Swedish Insurance Agency depersonalisation and responsibilisation in connection with digitalisation and reform of public agencies in Sweden (Bengtsson et al., 2023).

From the Magical Creature 'Kratt' to a Personalised State: The Case of Estonia

The wider discussions about data, automation and the data welfare state started in Estonia in 2018. Back then, Estonia, renowned for its advanced digital society and e-governance excellence, introduced a strategy to position the country as a global leader in the utilisation of algorithms and AI (E-Estonia – National AI Strategy for 2019–2021 Gets a Kick-Off, 2019); the ideals and aims were comparable to those of Sweden, as explained in the previous section. Additionally, Estonia has expressed its intent to function as a potential testing ground for algorithmic or AI solutions, including digital care work, open for use by other governments.

Care

The ground for discussions on welfare automation was created long before the launch of first data-based, automated and AI-based solutions. Understanding these developments is crucial, as they set the stage for the evolution of digital care work in Estonia, which is designed to assist individuals with their everyday tasks and routines while also fostering positive attitudes toward digital systems.

Estonia has implemented several initiatives to establish its digital society. 'Tiger Leap', initiated in 1997 (Tiger Leap 1997–2007, 1997), focuses on the nationwide development of computer networks and internet accessibility. The technological platform 'X-road', established in 2001, interconnects the state's information systems. Virtual data embassies, introduced in 2017 first time in the world (Data Embassy – e-Estonia, 2021), aim to safeguard governmental services by operating from a public state cloud and remote servers in the event of cyberattacks or emergencies. Additionally, Estonia introduced e-residency in 2014 (e-residency of Estonia, 2024), further contributing to the development of its digital infrastructure. Nevertheless, our recent research reveals that datafication not only transformed citizen practices and public administration but also served as a branding tool, both domestically and internationally for the country (Tammpuu & Masso, 2018). This brand is embodied in ambitious goals and visions, evident in slogans such as 'Estonia's aspiration to become the first country globally where no (paper) documents are utilised' (Pau, 2018).

In Estonia, the term 'Kratt' serves as a metaphor for AI (Kratid Eesti Heaks, 2024), symbolising the potential benefits and inherent risks associated with new solutions. Rooted in Estonian national mythology, a Kratt is a mythical creature – a servant crafted from hay or old household items, requiring constant attention to prevent idleness. According to folklore, reviving a Kratt involves offering three drops of blood to the devil (Mihkelev, 2017). On the other hand, the kratt was a familiar, endearing figure to people, which is why using this metaphor was part of a strategic mundanisation plan of the digital care work. The goal was to make automated, algorithmic, and AI-based applications more understandable and trustworthy to the public and within public administration practices The 'Kratt' project (Kratid Eesti Heaks, 2024) is dedicated to identifying specific applications where AI and algorithms can enhance efficiency and service quality. Throughout this initiative, experts aim to formulate a future-oriented strategy for Estonia, outlining considerations and conditions necessary for the development of AI and algorithmic solutions (see Kratid Eesti Heaks, 2024). While Estonia has shared its broad success in digitalisation globally, the perceived challenges and risks associated with algorithmic solutions were not widely disclosed to the public, at least during the first years. Hence, our study has proven valuable in collecting the opinions, experiences, fears and perceived risks from both citizens and experts working in the private, public and third sectors.

In Estonia, in recent years, 'Kratid' – automated, algorithmic or AI-based solutions – have been implemented in the public sector about 120 times. About 60 public sector institutions have implemented projects with an AI component to make their work more efficient (Kratid Eesti Heaks, 2024). The fields of application are very broad, including some of the following examples: border control, mass digitisation and image recognition of Estonian photographic heritage (FOTIS), counting road user groups (Fyma), biometric facial recognition for notarial transactions, predicting the health and treatment needs of the chronically ill patients, etc. Besides, a Bürokratt, a network of chatbots embedded in the websites of public sector institutions, has been established. It enables individuals to obtain information from these institutions through a chat window featuring spoken language communication (Kaun & Männiste, forthcoming).

In addition to these initiatives, various components of 'Kratt' are in use – the fundamental building blocks of AI applications that can be freely reused and further developed by all interested parties in the public and private sectors. An example includes an anonymiser, which can identify personal data entities from text, such as people's names, social security codes, dates and locations. However, as of 2022–2023, the new national plan for AI emphasises a renewed focus on 'data as enablers' (Estonia's National Artificial Intelligence Strategy or Kratt Strategy for 2022–2023, 2021). The objective is to enhance the findability, reusability and quality of data in both private and public sectors. In the private sector, efforts are directed towards increasing awareness of the potential of AI to enhance value in companies and supporting capable companies interested in developing and testing AI-based solutions. Additionally, in education and research and development, there is an increased emphasis on developing competence and skills and access to a world-class supercomputer resource for Estonia.

From these extensive examples, the labour market sector has gained significant attention, often recognised as one of the initial success stories of the digital care ork. Additionally, it offers valuable comparison opportunities with Sweden and Germany, the other cases discussed in this book, to explain the use of automated tools for the care purposes. The decision support system, OTT, employed by the unemployment fund, utilises a machine learning model trained on the employment data of the past five years to provide a comprehensive summary of an individual's situation. This includes predicting the likelihood of the person finding employment within the year, the probability of facing unemployment again and identifying relevant influencing factors, similar to the Swedish case. This enables counsellors to quickly assess their clients' situations and prioritise assistance based on individual needs. Furthermore, advisor managers leverage OTT assessments to evenly distribute workloads among advisors and provide additional support for complex client portfolios.

As the studies have indicated (see Turnbull, 2022), users of the OTT, including career counsellors, appreciate the perceived simplification of their work, providing them with a sense of clarity and purpose. The management sees success in data-based tools, attributing it to predefined rules of probability. However, questions arise about the emphasis on output and the true value of these considerations. While political interests align with reducing unemployment numbers, individuals and citizens may question the actual achievements and their value. The study suggests that the value might lie not just in the output but in the process itself.

Frictions

The promise of offering the best service to citizens is a major goal of OTT designers, but real constraints on users concerning the lives of public citizens (Turnbull, 2022). Users accept the AI's design and experience artificial objectives, but also raise concerns about the impact on citizens' lives. The unique aspect of this use case is that the AI system not only operates within an artificial world of citizen data but also defines the abilities and predefined future obstacles for citizens, such as re-entering unemployment. The AI becomes a decision-maker, matching citizens with jobs or training based on scores and probabilities, potentially offering relief from the perceived harsh realities of the world. However, this mediated reality may contribute to users seeking refuge in a world of predetermined decisions, where problems are clear and calculable. In the broader context of ongoing technological alterations and AI's ability to track and judge behaviour, the possibilities for modifications seem limitless. As an expert in the interviews expressed (Turnbull, 2022):

> I have not quite trusted the system in the beginning... and have not taken too much information, respectively which were already available to me before. That is, most of the time, or rather the first weeks, I did my usual work and at the same time. Ehh... I worked on the cases with the OTT and mostly still used my own estimation to work on them. Relatively many details were better or more extensively better solved and recognized by the system. (Interview conducted with a caseworker) (Turnbull, 2022)

Therefore, prior studies have identified key ideals related to the implementation of algorithmic systems, addressing concerns from various perspectives such as public interest, human rights, ethics and epistemology (Latzer & Just, 2020). From a public interest standpoint, risks associated with algorithmic applications include manipulation, threats to data protection and privacy (Pasquale, 2015), social discrimination (O'Neil, 2017), violation of intellectual property rights (Colangelo & Torti, 2019) and increasing human dependence on algorithms (Danaher, 2018). These concerns highlight the need for not only systematic risk assessment but also appropriate governance responses as these practices are mobilised to maximise economic and social welfare (Latzer & Just, 2020).

Failures

Another set of ideals related to digital care work, besides public interest, focuses on collective and individual human rights that may be violated by algorithmic decision-making (Latzer & Just, 2020). Therefore, frictions in the objectives and actual implementations can, in certain cases, lead to issues such as distrust, which may complicate the implementation of solutions. Discussions revolve around issues like racial bias in data-driven policing (Ferguson, 2017), regulation by algorithms of lived experience and identities (Cheney-Lippold, 2017) and data discrimination in search engine algorithms, emphasising the need to implement universal human rights principles and ideals in algorithmic governance. Human rights form the basis for ethical debates about the consequences of automation (Jaume-Palasí & Spielkamp, 2017). The focus on ethical conflicts in algorithmic processes underscores the collective nature of discrimination and the importance of addressing collective rights and access to collective goods (Jaume-Palasí & Spielkamp, 2017). Epistemic ideals express concerns about the quality of evidence gathered by algorithms, emphasising the need for traceability of cause and responsibility for harm (Latzer & Just, 2020). Concerns related to informational privacy, autonomy and moral responsibility arise from the potential inconclusive, inscrutable and error-prone nature of algorithmic evidence (Eubanks, 2018).

Transparency and accountability, closely intertwined with other ideals, play a crucial role in algorithmic governance debates (Ananny & Crawford, 2018; Lyon, 2018; Pasquale, 2015). The shift from rule-based to machine learning algorithms poses challenges regarding transparency and opacity, especially within already-opaque governance structures (Danaher et al., 2017). Calls for greater transparency assume that more information disclosure leads to increased trust and accountability (Albu & Flyverbom, 2016). However, the burden on individuals to seek and interpret information is acknowledged, highlighting the importance of meaningful transparency (Ananny & Crawford, 2018; Fung et al., 2007).

These ideals – encompassing public interest, human rights, ethics, epistemology, transparency and accountability – are considered some of the essential elements supporting the legitimacy of algorithmic governance, as we also have seen in the interviews we have conducted with experts being responsible for developing data-based solutions in Estonia, including both the public and private sector, and in collaboration of these sectors:

> It should be transparent for the decider. /.../ If the method itself is a so-called black box method from which nothing can be seen through /.../ the creator of the algorithm has no confidence about what basis this decision was made on. Perhaps it learnt totally insignificant features. (INT12, third sector)

> The algorithms must be transparent. Or when a certain decision is made that, in the end, a person is responsible. Or, at least ideally, it should be so that if there are decisions that influence people or their lives to a significant extent, it would be good if a person is liable for this decision. (INT12, third sector)

Therefore, studies conducted in Estonia reveal not only some adaptations but also discrepancies between initial ideals and actual applications. While experimental solutions may explain some discrepancies, certain areas, like the labour market, have already implemented practices. In response to potential risks, the principles of 'human-centred government' (Bason & Austin, 2022) have been recently formulateds to balance potential frictions and avoid failures in digital care work. These principles encompass respect for human dignity and autonomy, equal treatment and justice, job security and safety, transparency, responsibility and social and environmental well-being.

Conclusion

The implementation of data-based systems not only encompasses technical infrastructure and workflow organisation but also involves processes of constructing meaning. These meaning-making processes are encapsulated by the concept of mundanisation, which denotes the development of everyday relationships with complex technical systems. Part of mundanisation entails the development of definitions and understandings of what a specific technology is and what it does. In delving into this question of technology's nature and function, this chapter explores the practices of mundanisation that contribute to the stabilisation of socio-technical imaginaries, going beyond the emphasis on the influential roles of specific actors. Emphasising the perspective of mundanisation underscores the significance of subtle yet impactful actions concerning emerging technologies and infrastructures. Adopting this perspective also allows for moving beyond the discussion of scandals around algorithmic automation in the context of welfare provision that obscures the important ways in which especially vulnerable populations are impacted by the introduction of data-based systems and AI for decision-making.

Digital care work and phatic labour are part of the mundanisation process and highlight specific practices, that is, how mundanisation is done actively. Being active promoters of digitalisation, for example, in the role as digital ambassadors, constitutes important mundane ways of translating large-scale national strategies into concrete practices. They also constitute what could be considered as lubricants of automation projects. Though mundane and seemingly small, they make implementation projects possible. The various examples of implementation projects in Sweden and Estonia discussed in this chapter highlight these important practices.

References

Albu, O. B., & Flyverbom, M. (2016). Organizational transparency: Conceptualizations, conditions, and consequences. *Business & Society*. http://doi.org/10.1177/0007650316659851

Ananny, M., & Crawford, K. (2018). Seeing without knowing: Limitations of the transparency ideal and its application to algorithmic accountability. *New Media & Society*, *20*(3), 973–989.

Arbetsförmedling. (2021a). Träffsäkerhet och likabehandling vid automatiserade anvisningar inom Rusta och matcha. Dnr: Af-2020/0046 7913, Arbetsförmedlingen analys 2021:9.

Arbetsförmedling. (2021b). *Kundval Rusta och Matcha – Uppföljning och lärdomar efter ett år med en ny matchningstjänst*. Dnr: Af-2021/0037 4739, Arbetsförmedlingen analys 2021:15.

Arcy, J. (2016) Emotion work: Considering gender in digital labor. *Feminist Media Studies*, 16(2), 365–368. http://doi.org/10.1080/14680777.2016.1138609

Bason, C., & Austin, R. D. (2022). Design in the public sector: Toward a human centred model of public governance. *Public Management Review*, 24(11), 1727–1757. https://doi.org/10.1080/14719037.2021.1919186

Bengtsson, M., Jacobsson, K., & Wallinder, Y. (2023). A journey into the new employment service landscape of responsibilisation: Towards de-personalisation of the caseworker–jobseeker relationship. *International Journal of Social Welfare*, 1–14. https://doi.org/10.1111/ijsw.12584

Bowker, G., & Leigh Star, S. (1999). *Sorting things out: Classification and its consequences*. MIT Press.

Carlsson, V. (2023). Legal certainty in automated decision-making in welfare services. *Public Policy and Administration*. https://doi.org/10.1177/09520767231202334

Cheney-Lippold, J. (2017). *We are data: Algorithms and the making of our digital selves*. New York University Press.

Choroszewicz, M., & Mäihäniemi, B. (2020). Developing a digital welfare state: Data protection and the use of automated decision-making in the public sector across six EU countries. *Global Perspectives*, 1(1), 12910.

Colangelo, G., & Torti, V. (2019). Copyright, online news publishing and aggregators: A law and economics analysis of the EU reform. *International Journal of Law and Info Technology*, 27(1), 75–90.

Danaher, J. (2018). Toward an ethics of AI assistants: An initial framework. *Philosophy & Technology*, 31(4), 629–653.

Danaher, J., Hogan, M. J., Noone, C., Kennedy, R., Behan, A., De Paor, A., Felzmann, H., Haklay, M., Khoo, S. M., Morison, J., Murphy, M. H., O'Brolchain, N., Schafer, B., & Shankar, K. (2017). Algorithmic governance: Developing a research agenda through the power of collective intelligence. *Big Data & Society*, 4(2), https://doi.org/10.1177/2053951717726554

Data Embassy—E-Estonia. (2021, October 20). https://e-estonia.com/solutions/e-governance/data-embassy/

E-Estonia—national AI strategy for 2019-2021 gets a kick-off. (2019). https://e-estonia.com/nationa-ai-strategy/

Elyachar, J. (2010). Phatic labor, infrastructure, and the question of empowerment in Cairo. *American Ethnologist*, 37(3), 452-464.

Estonia's national artificial intelligence strategy or Kratt Strategy for 2022–2023. (2021). https://www.kratid.ee/_files/ugd/980182_4434a890f1e64c66b1190b0bd2665dc2.pdf

Eubanks, V. (2018). *Automating inequality: How high-tech tools profile, police, and punish the poor* (1st ed.). St. Martin's Press.

Ferguson, A. G. (2017). *The rise of big data policing: Surveillance, race, and the future of law enforcement*. NYU Press.

Fung, A., Graham, M., & Weil, D. (2007). *Full disclosure: The perils and promise of transparency*. Cambridge University Press.

Gitelman, L. (2008). *Always already new. Media, history, and the data of culture*. MIT Press.
IAF. (2021). Fungerar Arbetsförmedlingens kontroll av aktivitetsrapporter? Rapport 2021:12.
IFAU. (2021). KROM – Erfarenheter från en matchningstjänst med fristående leverantörer inom arbetsmarknadspolitiken. https://www.ifau.se/Forskning/Publikationer/Rapporter/20212/krom–erfarenheter-fran-en-ny-matchningstjanst-med-fristaende-leverantorer-inom-arbetsmarknadspolitiken/
Jarrett, K. (2016) *Feminism, labour and digital media: The digital housewife*. Routledge.
Jaume-Palasí, L. &, Spielkamp, M. (2017). *Ethics and algorithmic processes for decision making and decision support*. AlgorithmWatch Working Paper No. 2, Berlin. https://algorithmwatch.org/wp-content/uploads/2017/06/AlgorithmWatch_Working-Paper_No_2_Ethics_ADM.pdf
Kalm, S. (2019). Om akademiskt hushållsarbete och dess fördelning. *Sociologisk Forskning*, 6(1), 5–26.
Kaun, A. (2022). Suing the algorithm: The mundanization of automated decision-making in public services through litigation. *Information, Communication & Society*, 25(14), 2046–2062.
Kaun and Männiste. (forthcoming). Public sector chatbots: AI frictions and data infrastructures for equality and human flourishing? *New Media & Society*.
Kaun, A., & Forsman, M. (2024). Digital care work at public libraries: Making Digital First possible. *New Media & Society*, 26(7), 3751–3766.
Kratid Eesti Heaks (2024). http://www.kratid.ee/
Latzer, M., & Just, N. (2020). *Governance by and of algorithms on the internet: Impact and consequences*. Oxford Research Encyclopedia of Communication. https://doi.org/10.1093/acrefore/9780190228613.013.904
Lindberg, A. (2021). Arbetsförmedling går vidare med omdiskuterat AI-test. Dagens nyheter 2021-05-07.
Lyon, D. (2018). *The culture of surveillance: Watching as a way of life*. Polity Press.
Mihkelev, A. (2017). Folk tradition and multimedia in contemporary Estonian culture. *Philologia Estonica Tallinnensis*, 2, 108–128. https://doi.org/10.22601/pet.2017.02.06
Mol, A., Moser, I., & Pols, J. (Eds.). (2010). *Care in practice: On tinkering in clinics, homes and farms*. Transcript Verlag.
Morley, D., & Silverstone, R. (1990). Domestic communication – technologies and meanings. *Media, Culture & Society*, 12(1), 31-55.
Neyland, D. (2019). *The everyday life of an algorithm* (p. 151). Springer Nature.
O'Neil, C. (2017). *Weapons of math destruction: How big data increases inequality and threatens democracy*. Crown.
Pasquale, F. (2015). *The black box society: The secret algorithms that control money and information*. Harvard University Press.
Pau, A. (2018). *Kuhu on kadunud 20 000 e-residenti?* [Where have gone 20 000 e-residents] Postimees, September 16, electronically available at: https://tehnika.postimees.ee/6406321/kuhu-on-kadunud-20-000-e-residenti?_ga=2.58464495.437348784.1537001581-373652059.1533898534. Accessed on September 16.
Peters, J. D. (2015). *The marvellous Clouds. Towards a philosophy of elemental media*. The University of Chicago Press.

Pink, S., Ruckenstein, M., Berg, M., & Lupton, D. (2022). Everyday automation: Setting a research agenda. *Everyday automation*, 1–19.
Puig de la Bellacasa, M. (2010) Matters of care in technoscience: Assembling neglected things. *Social Studies of Science, 41*(1), 85–106.
Rakar, F. (2018). *Lärprojekt Trelleborgsmodellen – Från Rebell till Modell* [Project Trelleborg model – From rebel to model]. www.moten.trelleborg.se/arbetsmarknadsnamnden/agenda
Regeringen. (2023). Kommittédirektiv: Förstärkt AI-förmåga i Sverige. https://www.regeringen.se/rattsliga-dokument/kommittedirektiv/2023/12/dir.-2023164
Ruckenstein, M. (2023). *The feel of algorithms*. Univ of California Press.
Silverstone, R. (2005). Domesticating domestication. Reflections on the life of a concept. In T. Berker, M. Hartmann, Y. Punie, & K. J. Ward (Eds.), *Domestication of media and technology* (pp. 229–248). Open University Press.
Singh, R. (2024). Intermediaries as infrastructure: Interrogating the phatic labor of state-building. *Journal of Sociology*, https://doi.org/10.1177/14407833241234675.
Star, S. L. & Ruhleder, K. (1996). Steps towards an ecology of infrastructure: Design and access for large information spaces. In: *Information Systems Research 7*(1), 111–124.
Sveriges Television. (2018). Mer bidragstagare fick jobb när robot tog over ansökningar om stöd [More recipients of social benefits got jobs when a robot took over applications for support]. https://sverigesradio.se/artikel/6856831
Tammpuu, P., & Masso, A. (2018). 'Welcome to the virtual state': Estonian e-residency and the digitalised state as a commodity. *European Journal of Cultural Studies, 21*(5), 543–560. https://doi.org/10.1177/1367549417751148
Tiger Leap 1997-2007. (1997). https://www.educationestonia.org/wp-content/uploads/2023/01/tiigrihype2007ENG_standard.pdf
Tronto, J. C. (1993) *Moral boundaries: A political argument for an ethic of care*. Routledge.
Tronto, J., & Fisher, B. (1990). Toward a feminist theory of caring. In E. K. Abel & M. K. Nelson (Eds.), *Circles of care: Work and identity in women's lives* (pp. 36–54). State University of New York.
Turnbull, S. D. (2022). *How does the use of technology in innovative public services influence the way we relate to the world around us? A case study on the use of artificial intelligence in Labour Market services*. Master Thesis, Ragnar Nurkse Department of Innovation and Governance (supervisor A. Masso, A.Moktefi), https://digikogu.taltech.ee/et/item/d5d8826c-557d-466d-bdfc-892dfcdd0120
Willim, R. (2017). Imperfect imaginaries: Digitisation, mundanisation, and the ungraspableIn G. Koch (Ed.), *Digitisation: Theories and concepts for empirical cultural research* (pp. 53–77). Routledge.
Willim, R. (2019). *From a talk at: Man or machine? Who will decide in the future*. Paper presented at the Future Week at Lund University, Lund.

3
Experiences of Data Welfare

Scene: Sara confronts a digital judgment in Stockholm. In Stockholm's quiet streets, Sara faced an unsettling intrusion when an automated child welfare system assessed her family. A letter, bearing the weight of digital judgment, revealed a risk score crafted from her family's background, education, and neighbourhood crime rates. As Sara opened the letter, a numerical oracle unfolded the next steps – a looming home visit and interviews orchestrated by an unseen force. The predictive algorithm, devoid of empathy, aimed to safeguard the vulnerable child. Yet, it left Sara grappling with the question: Can a calculated risk score truly understand the intricacies of her family's dynamics?

In this chapter, we focus on the experiences of the data welfare state as it emerges for citizens who interact with automated systems, digital platforms and communicative artificial intelligence (AI; including chatbots) to interact with the public administration.

The chapter relies mainly on representative surveys conducted in Estonia, Germany and Sweden ($N = 4501$) to capture a range of experiences with AI implementation. It particularly emphasises the awareness of automation in the public sector, perceived risks and trust in and values related to automated decision-making (ADM) in the welfare sector, based on citizens' views. The questionnaire authors developed for this survey was distributed to a representative sample in each country in collaboration with Kantar Sifo, an opinion and social research company that utilises online population panels. The survey targeted individuals aged 18–75, with the final research sample consisting of 1,500 participants in Estonia, 2,001 in Germany and 1,000 in Sweden (see Table 3.1). The response rates were between 15 and 16%, which is similar to response rates observed in online panels compared to face-to-face surveys, a comparison made against face-to-face surveys (Szolnoki & Hoffmann, 2013) and studies relying on respondents from paid crowdsourcing (Eklund et al., 2019). Participants, when completing the web survey, averaged a completion time of 15 minutes. The surveys were administered in local languages, with translation validity assured through a two-way translation, multiple testing and rigorous examination of study instruments by participants in the three countries.

Table 3.1 Sample Structure of the Survey (%)

		Estonia	Germany	Sweden	Total
Gender	Male	51	49	51	50
	Female	49	52	49	50
Age	18–34	26	39	39	34
	35–49	37	38	29	35
	59–75	37	23	32	31
Place of residence	A large city	44	29	24	32
	A suburb of a big city	8	14	16	13
	A small- or medium-sized city	25	36	39	33
	Village	14	19	21	18
	Farm or home in the countryside	9	2	0	4
Total	%	100	100	100	100
	N	1,500	2001	1,000	4501

Based on the survey data, this chapter explores the evolving state-citizen relations from citizens' perspectives and examines how the state and welfare provision are perceived as they become increasingly mediated through digital platforms and automated systems. The chapter also discusses the ambivalent development of trust based on this mediation, which is strengthened for certain groups while others increasingly distrust the state. We specifically focus on three key variables – awareness, trust, risk perception and suitability assessment – as well as values, which emerged in our analysis as the most significant indicators characterising the nature of relationships between individuals and the state in the context of the adoption of ADM in public administration institutions.

To demonstrate the differences and similarities within and between countries with various welfare traditions, we have developed an original typology based on these indicators. This typology allows for a more precise explanation of the diverse ways in which ADM might be perceived among different population groups, and consequently, it also assesses the extent to which these solutions are applicable, considering potential acceptance or resistance by individuals. A typological approach has proven to be a suitable tool in our previous studies (Kalmus et al., 2020), enabling to make of latent mechanisms in how citizens adapt to changes visible. Explaining these latent mechanisms is particularly important in contexts where many mechanisms of change are non-linear and cannot be explained purely quantitatively. By combining factor and cluster analysis techniques, which allow us to aggregate a large number of indicators and analyse their interrelationships, we have developed a typology for adapting to ADM.

We will next explain why we should care about peoples' attitudes towards the data welfare state and the automation of welfare, and examine individual indicators such as risk perception, awareness, suitability and trust, as well as values related to the data welfare state. Finally, we will introduce the typology developed based on these individual indicators for adapting to the automation of welfare.

Why Should Citizens Care About the Data Welfare State?

The data welfare state, implementing different data-based technologies including ADM, is increasingly scrutinised by not only research but also civil society as we will see in the next chapter as well. Particularly noteworthy in current research is the shift away from the traditional confines of computer science, as the implementation of the General Data Protection Regulation (GDPR) ('General Data Protection Regulation (EU) 2016/679,' 2016) has driven an expansion of studies into the realms of social sciences and humanities. This research has predominantly revolved around themes of governance and regulation (Binns, 2018; Borgesius, 2020; Larsson, 2020; Wagner et al., 2023), values and ethics (Masso et al., 2023; Veale & Edwards, 2018) and, but less frequently, the individuals engaged in the implementation process (Brown et al., 2019; Dencik et al., 2018; Lomborg et al., 2023). The latter part of this research has primarily focused on those responsible for developing ADM solutions (Henriksen & Blond, 2023), the workers underpinning ADM infrastructures (Wu, 2023) and labourers operating at the interfaces of ADM solutions (Ranerup & Svensson, 2023).

Within specific domains, there has been a growing interest in studying the welfare and public sectors (Eubanks, 2018; Henriksen & Blond, 2023; Reutter, 2022), with a particular emphasis on shifts in the discretion of case workers and their agency in relation to ADM systems. Moreover, studies have shed light on the socio-technical imaginaries of policymakers, the public sector and technology businesses serving the public sector (Hockenhull & Cohn, 2021; Jørgensen & Søe, 2023). More attention has been directed towards universal hard and soft laws governing ADM in the public sector. Previous research has also demonstrated that citizens differentiate between various domains and purposes for which ADM is deployed (Kaun et al., 2023), a distinction that can significantly influence how public agencies and state representatives deploying ADM are perceived, particularly in terms of not only trust but also values (Masso et al., 2023). There has been relatively limited research on the role and perspective of citizens regarding ADM systems, with Araujo et al., 2020 serving as a notable exception. In their work, the authors examine citizens' preferences for governmental use of AI and contribute to the study of what they term 'algorithmic appreciation', which highlights citizen perceptions beyond mere utility. Furthermore, if we consider ADM as a political issue, not solely a managerial one (Reutter, 2022), then citizen perspectives become crucial for shaping the future of the digital welfare state and determining how ADM should be governed. Therefore, recent research has gone further (Kasapoglu et al., 2021; Kasapoglu & Masso, 2021; Masso & Kasapoglu, 2020), suggesting that only a systematic comparison of the views of data subjects and experts targeted by these automated solutions will help unlock changes in public welfare services concerning automation.

The emergence of the data welfare state has also increasingly been framed as a political issue that requires the engagement of citizens. Advocacy groups such as AlgorithmWatch have actively worked towards highlighting AI and ADM in the public domain as a political question. Part of this work has been a request for more transparency as well as explainability of both actors involved in the automation process as well as the technologies themselves. Understanding how a specific data-based, algorithmic system is working, the argument enables critical engagement by citizens who are implicated in and affected by it. There have been several attempts at operationalising transparency of algorithmic systems in the public sector through, for example, registries of algorithms in use. Given the diverse traditions in welfare sector development and the varied implementation of automated solutions across countries, along with distinct norms, understandings and values regarding welfare automation, the subsequent review and analysis concentrate on comparing three countries: Estonia, Germany and Sweden.

It is assumed that the data welfare state might be perceived as a relatively abstract concept, not always experienced directly by individuals. Nevertheless, the topic has gained public attention, particularly with the emergence of ChatGPT and other large language models exemplifying how the use of artificial intelligence applications have reached broader audiences, becoming a routine tool in daily work. Our qualitative studies support the assumption that people have had relatively close encounters with this field. Even when individuals lack direct interaction with automated solutions or haven't experienced data welfare applications in their dealings with state authorities, the topic has garnered public attention. Consequently, ordinary citizens have formed attitudes, opinions and perceptions regarding these emerging innovations.

How Do Citizens Care?

Through a population-representative survey in Germany, Estonia and Sweden, we have documented citizens' attitudes, experiences and future visions for the data welfare state (see Table 3.1 for the sample structure of the survey). In addition, we have conducted in-depth interviews with citizens who are especially vulnerable to algorithmic automation within the data welfare state including long-term unemployed (see also Chapters 2 and 4).

Citizens' experiences with and attitudes towards the data welfare state are notoriously difficult to capture. The algorithmic system and data-based tools implemented in the data welfare state are increasingly surrounded by an aura of complexity and black-boxness. Additionally, these solutions are frequently contextualised within the economic considerations and ideals associated with neoliberalism. They tend to align with the norms of efficiency and effectiveness in public administration, as well as the ideals of digitalisation reform. These strategies have also frequently been employed in both internal and external country branding. This has been particularly appealing to Estonia, an independent and small nation seeking to establish and demonstrate its position on the international stage, albeit for a relatively short period. Therefore, one way to unlock these hidden complexities is to focus on the issues of awareness, trust, risk perception and enthusiasm regarding the state of data well-being expressed by citizens in different countries. This is the path we have taken in our empirical research, and it has proven fruitful.

Awareness and Suitability

First, we explain the awareness and perceived suitability of data-based applications in the welfare sector, based on citizens' perspectives in three countries: Estonia, Germany and Sweden (Kaun et al., 2023). As we have measured the citizen's attitudes and understandings using detailed and single variables, we have seen, based on our previous experiences and research on comparative studies (Kalmus et al., 2020; Schlüter et al., 2019), that calculating the compound index variables has been the most fruitful approach to measure the complex phenomena like attitudes towards data welfare. The following synthesised overview is derived from an analysis of these index variables and is grounded in a conducted empirical study (Kaun et al., 2023). We operationalised data welfare primarily as forms of automated decision-making (ADM) that presupposed digitalisation and datafication of work processes within public agencies.

As depicted in Figure 3.1, Germans demonstrate a greater awareness of ADM compared to both Estonians and Swedes. However, at the same time, German respondents are also characterised by a slightly higher heterogeneity in the answers – more people have given very high or very low ratings (see standard deviations in Figure 3.1). Interestingly, no significant difference in awareness was observed between the latter two countries – citizens in Sweden and Estonia express rather similar but lower awareness compared to citizens in Germany in ADM. Specifically, the results from Estonia yielded a mean of 1.6, while the average for Swedish respondents was reported as 1.58. Although in the case of Estonia and Sweden awareness of ADM is somewhat lower, the respondents are characterised by a slightly smaller dispersion of answers – citizens' opinions have been somewhat more unanimous compared to those surveyed in Germany.

Another index variable analysed here is the perceived and estimated suitability of ADM tools and approaches within each country. As the results in Figure 3.1b highlight, our Estonian respondents stand out as the most enthusiastic towards ADM, placing them at the forefront. Meanwhile, their German and Swedish counterparts find

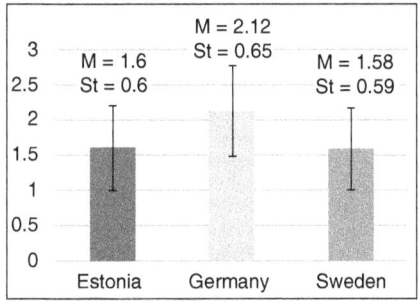 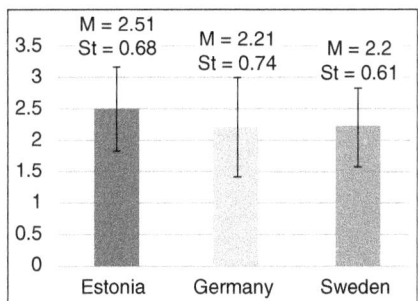

Figure 3.1 Citizens' Awareness (A) and Their Perception of Suitability (B) Concerning Automated Decision-Making in Public Administration (Mean and Standard Deviation)
Source: Authors' figure based on Kaun et al. (2023).

themselves in a shared runner-up position (the mean values in Germany and Sweden were not statistically significant, $p > 0.001$). However, like the variation observed in awareness of ADM, individual responses in Germany exhibit greater variability compared to the other two countries.

The higher awareness among Germans could be attributed to their longer traditions in public discussions (Schmidt & Weichert, 2012) about the implementation of data technologies and the associated potential issues related to privacy and other legal implications. However, the larger variability suggests that it may still be a topic that generates numerous controversial views and discussions. Consensus or publicly shared views on this matter might still be in the process of development. On the other hand, the high assessment of Estonians regarding the suitability of ADM may be linked to the integration of automated and digital solutions into everyday life. These technologies have become closely intertwined with routine practices that are accepted without much thought, potentially leading people to overlook whether they are aware of the changes. In such cases, these technologies might no longer be perceived as something new deserving special attention.

Although one might have assumed that a higher level of agreement with ADM, stemming from people's interactions or mediated experiences with these solutions, would also be accompanied by a greater awareness of both ADM solutions and their associated benefits and risks, the subsequent analysis revealed that awareness of automated systems and consent to them are not necessarily correlated.

Thus, based on the evaluation of awareness and suitability, we can conditionally categorise our respondents into three groups: (1) those with a high level of awareness but a low assessment of suitability, (2) those with low awareness but a high assessment of suitability and (3) those with a relatively similar, mid-level assessment of suitability and awareness. Let us provisionally label these types as 'the wild natives of ADM' (example of Estonia), 'informed sceptics' (example of Germany) and 'agreeing conformists' (example of Sweden). We acknowledge that these designations are only provisional and intentionally exaggerated. However, we employ these labels to generalise distinct tendencies that may recur, to some extent, albeit with varying emphases, in countries that share similar patterns of experience with ADM. Additionally, although at first glance it may seem that we can distinguish people's readiness and attitudes towards ADM by country and according to different welfare models, the following analysis delves deeper into the differences not only between countries but also within them. We will see that the picture is significantly more complex than this tripartite division suggests.

Trust in Automated Decision-Making

In addition to awareness and suitability assessments, we have found that trust in both national institutions and ADM is a significant factor that differentiates the three analysed countries and their citizens. Trust is one of the most important indicators analysed, as the state cannot create and implement technological solutions without the trust of its citizens, even if these solutions function well (Masso & Kasapoglu, 2020; Männiste & Masso, 2018).

Drawing on previous studies (Kalmus et al., 2020; Vihalemm et al., 2017), we recognise that trust serves as a potential factor in elucidating people's sense of connection to the state overall and to state institutions in particular. Moreover, trust has proven to be a reliable characteristic for analysing various changes (*ibid*.), including the convergence of opinions regarding the implementation and adoption of automated solutions in state institutions. Like the previous subsection, we have also computed index values here. We summed up the results of individual questions to better generalise the tendencies of well-being by country and by model. Assuming that trust in the transition to ADM may be linked to general trust in state institutions, we have next analysed these two dimensions (see also Kaun et al., 2023).

In general, based on Figure 3.2a, we can observe that while there is no clear distinction between respondents from Estonia and Sweden regarding trust in ADM, both countries report relatively higher levels of trust compared to German respondents. More in detail, statistical tests (Chi-square and Cramer's V) indicated that the means, as well as variations in the means, for Sweden and Estonia, were not significantly different from each other ($p >= 0.001$). This suggests that citizens in Sweden and Estonia express somewhat higher but also consensual trust in ADM.

In the case of Estonians, we must consider that state institutions have undergone fundamental changes. In a situation where most national institutions were rebuilt in the early 1990s, restoring people's trust in these institutions was imperative. For Sweden, the phenomenon lies in the country's ideals of equality, fostering a sense that individuals are considered and included. The presence of strong trade unions also contributes, allowing people to easily approach institutions in everyday situations. In the case of Germany, it may not be so much about direct mistrust but rather caution, reflection and criticism of the activities of national institutions.

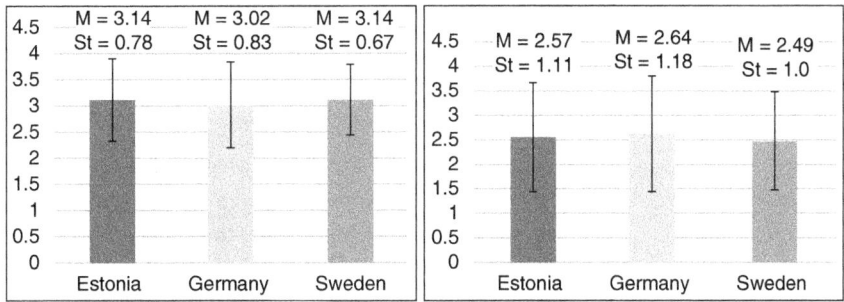

Figure 3.2 Citizens' Trust in Societal Institutions (A) and Automated Decision-Making (B) in Public Administration (Mean and Standard Deviation)
Source: Authors' figure based on Kaun et al. (2023).

Compared to trust in societal actors, illustrated in Figure 3.2a, trust in ADM exhibited some differences and similarities across the three studied countries. Germany led the rankings ($m = 2.64$), closely followed by Estonia ($m = 2.57$), while Swedish respondents displayed the least amount of trust ($m = 2.49$) in this context (see Figure 3.2b). However, these estimates are quite similar regarding awareness of ADM. Besides, the data indicate that the higher the average value of the evaluations, the greater the deviation from the average. Behind the high opinions of Germany, there are internally very heterogeneous evaluations.

However, as these differences were not statistically significant ($p >= 0.001$), we can conclude that there are no discernible variations in trust in ADM between the three countries. Yet, an intriguing inconsistency arises between respondent trust in societal actors and trust in ADM. While German respondents expressed the least trust towards societal actors, they also exhibited the highest – although not significantly so – level of trust in ADM. It is worth noting that, when comparing the findings presented in Figure 3.2, the mean levels of trust in societal actors tend to be slightly higher than the mean levels of trust in ADM.

Therefore, based on these results, we can conclude that trust in ADM is not necessarily correlated with trust in public institutions. Metaphorically, 'informed sceptics' (as exemplified by Germany), who lack trust in state institutions, may look to ADM tools as a new source of trust. Conversely, 'the wild natives of automated decision-making' (as exemplified by Estonia), who do trust traditional institutions, express somewhat lower trust in ADM. This can be explained by the notion that solutions integrated into everyday life are not perceived as something new or distinct from the daily routine operations of public administration. In the case of 'agreeing conformists' (as exemplified by Sweden), trust in both state institutions and automated solutions is relatively comparable, reflecting a general characteristic of people's connection to the state.

Risk Perception

The third dimension examined in our study, which we found to be crucial in shaping readiness for ADM, pertains to the perception of risk (see also Kaun et al., 2023). In the context of risk perception associated with ADM in public administration, an analysis of variance revealed significant mean differences among the three countries under study ($p < 0.001$). This suggests that while Swedish respondents ($m = 4.33$), followed closely by Estonian respondents ($m = 4.19$), were more likely to perceive risk in this context, respondents from Germany ($m = 3.88$) tended to view ADM as less risky. Nevertheless, as depicted in Figure 3.3 by the standard deviations, a noteworthy trend emerges: the higher the perceived risk concerning automation, the smaller the variation within the population. This implies that while Estonians and Swedes exhibit greater sensitivity to risk, these cautious attitudes are widespread and unanimous across the majority of their populations. In contrast, among Germans who perceive lower risks, there exists a broader spectrum, with both highly risk-sensitive and minimally sensitive citizens within the population.

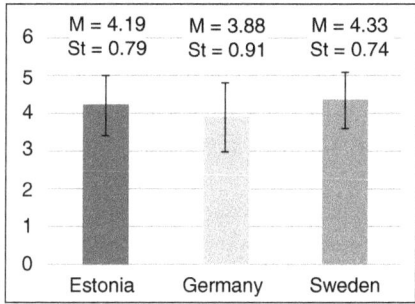

Figure 3.3 Risk Perception of Automated Decision-Making in Public Administration (Mean and Standard Deviation)
Source: Authors' figure based on Kaun et al. (2023).

Based on this analysis, we can conclude that 'informed sceptics' (Germany), having considered various perspectives regarding the usability of ADM, have gained confidence in these solutions, resulting in a lower perception of risk. In contrast, 'wild natives' (Estonia) and 'agreeing conformists' (Sweden), where such open discussions in society may have been less prevalent, exhibit somewhat higher levels of risk perception. However, from these analyses, we can see that the issue may revolve around trust, suitability assessments and risk perception, which have developed according to societal discussions on acceptable norms and practices. Values also play a significant role – assessments of what is considered important in the development and use of automated solutions in the public sector. Therefore, the following subsection will delve into citizens' values in three countries regarding ADM.

It Is All About Values

Besides analysing trust and awareness, risk perception and perception of suitability in regard of ADM, our study revealed that people's concerns and their outcomes are often rooted in their value estimates and potential conflicts in these. These conflicts may arise between developers and users, as well as across different sectors where solutions are implemented. Subsequently, we analysed attitudes and evaluations regarding these conflicts, taking into account pressures from institutions and the essential criteria formulated by several institutions for developing and implementing various automated solutions (Hagendorff, 2020).

Our starting point in the analysis of values was that the rapid growth of AI systems' design and implementation raises unresolved issues related to AI alignment and control especially in the context of the data welfare state, particularly in ensuring systems aid rather than harm humans (see e.g. Masso & Kasapoglu, 2020). The use of various AI solutions is increasingly widespread in public administration organisations, where they are employed for ADM in the welfare sector, aiming to enhance efficiency and prudent resource allocation, thereby ensuring societal well-being (see also Chapter 1 for an overview of historical developments). Our assumption here was, based on Ibo van de Poel (see e.g. van de Poel, 2020), that there is a lack of coherence and common understanding regarding AI values by introducing original instruments to empirically test human evaluations of conflicting principles in AI system design, use and implementation.

While there is a widespread academic discussion on formulating, testing and adapting ethical guidelines for AI development (Hagendorff, 2020), conflicts in AI values persist. This includes tensions between explainability and environmental sustainability (König et al., 2022). Despite a global abundance of ethical guidelines, there is insufficient knowledge about why AI developers face social dilemmas, hindering the widespread adoption of ethical best practices (Strümke et al., 2021). Additionally, there is a lack of empirical knowledge about the embeddedness of values in AI artefacts and diverse social contexts (Helberger et al., 2020). Also, discussions on AI's social and political consequences often centre on ethical standards, but operationalising these demands into practice presents challenges (van de Poel, 2020). Developers must navigate personal values versus company goals, resulting in dynamic and changing understandings of values across domains, sectors, countries and individuals. However, understanding changing values at these levels is crucial for adapting to the development and implementation of AI.

While normative discussions on AI and values exist (Fatima et al., 2022; Wang, 2022; Wirtz & Müller, 2019; Züger & Asghari, 2022), there is a lack of measurable instruments to empirically gauge how citizens understand AI values formulated in normative guidelines. Existing studies on human values lack instruments to measure and explain value understandings embedded in AI artefacts (Han et al., 2022; Kasirzadeh & Gabriel, 2022; Umbrello, 2022), creating gaps and a need for empirical studies and conceptualisations, especially from a citizen perspective (van de Poel, 2020). Few studies focus explicitly on citizens' experiences with increased AI implementation, particularly in public administration and welfare provision contexts (Gesk & Leyer, 2022; Ingrams et al., 2022).

Our study aimed to fill this gap by proposing original survey instruments to measure citizens' understanding, agreement and disagreement with AI values articulated in moral guidelines (Hagendorff, 2020). Applying exploratory factor analysis, the study sought potential underlying dimensions of values based on citizens' correlations with constructed value items, contributing to discussions on the conceptual framework of basic values in AI. In our study, we formulated 15 items drawing on prior research, particularly the guidelines and principles (see e.g. Hagendorff, 2020) concerning values in automated solutions (see Table 3.2). We asked respondents to estimate how important they think these aspects are when AI solutions are developed, as a support tool in decision-making in public administration organisations.

The analysis results revealed that respondents generally perceived these listed 15 items often used in the AI development guidelines as significant, with mean values

Table 3.2 Descriptive Statistics of the Artificial Intelligence Values (Mean, Standard Deviation)*

	Estonia		Germany		Sweden		Total	
	m**	σ	m	σ	m	σ	m	σ
1. Efficiency (saving costs, time and similar resources)	3.76	0.89	3.25	1.01	3.49	0.95	3.47	0.98
2. Privacy (protection of personal data)	4.55	0.76	4.11	1.04	4.34	0.89	4.30	0.94
3. Diversity (e.g. consideration of ethnic, gender, lifestyle groups)	3.71	1.00	3.50	1.05	3.69	1.17	3.61	1.06
4. Justice (socially justified activities and decisions in relation to the data)	4.38	0.77	3.97	1.01	4.17	0.91	4.15	0.93
5. Equality (equal treatment of all data subjects, being the target of data solutions)	4.37	0.77	3.98	1.03	4.23	0.98	4.17	0.96
6. Accountability (responsibility for the use of data and possible consequences)	4.66	0.63	4.00	1.01	4.50	0.73	4.33	0.89
7. Transparency (openness and access to the data)	4.35	0.85	3.91	1.02	4.19	0.88	4.12	0.96
8. Security (including cyber security, reducing people's insecurity, ensuring a sense of security)	4.70	0.61	4.13	0.99	4.53	0.76	4.41	0.87
9. Welfare (benefits to society)	4.18	0.82	3.77	0.98	4.12	0.83	3.99	0.92
10. Sustainability (environmental protection, reduction of data waste)	4.11	0.87	3.68	1.09	3.89	1.06	3.87	1.03
11. Monitoring (effective control of human behaviour)	3.64	1.09	3.09	1.12	3.17	1.09	3.29	1.13
12. Solidarity (people involvement, social cohesion)	3.81	0.93	3.64	0.98	3.68	1.06	3.71	0.98
13. Explainability (interpretability of results, comprehensibility for people)	4.25	0.78	3.80	0.95	4.05	0.86	4.00	0.90
14. Autonomy (people's power to decide independently)	4.20	0.80	3.72	0.99	4.03	0.87	3.95	0.93
15. Interoperability (adaptability, transferability, cross-border, universal usability)	3.82	0.84	3.42	0.91	3.53	0.81	3.58	0.8

Source: Masso et al. (2023), Authors' calculations.
*Mean values on the 5-point scale: 1 – completely insignificant, 2 – rather insignificant, 3 – neither important nor insignificant, 4 – rather important, 5 – very important.
**Italics indicates the different mean values from standard deviations in the table
m, mean values; σ, standard deviation; ADM, automated decision-making; PA, public administration.

exceeding 4.16 on a scale where 4 signifies rather important and 5 signifies very important (see Table 3.2). This implies that citizens, the targeted recipients of AI system design and implementation, endorse the value criteria articulated in AI experts' ethical guidelines and regulations. Among the 15 values, six, including security, accountability, privacy, equality, justice and transparency, were deemed more significant with the least variation across individuals ($\sigma < 0.1$ in Table 3.2). These values are commonly included in AI ethics guidelines and have garnered more public attention. Explainability, welfare, autonomy and sustainability also received relatively high importance, with relatively low heterogeneity in responses. Conversely, solidarity, diversity, interoperability and efficiency were assigned the lowest importance, with the highest variation among respondents (standard deviation, σ, is around 0.1). This might be attributed to these values being less discussed in ethics guidelines and public discourse, possibly indicating a lack of understanding.

On the other hand, values like solidarity and diversity showed the smallest differences among the three countries, suggesting their embeddedness in the general understanding of human rights. The value of monitoring, reflecting the effective control of human behaviour, received the lowest estimates and the most controversial responses. The low importance may indicate awareness and public discussion of the negative outcomes of using AI for controlling human behaviour. The high standard deviations suggest varied interpretations, including control by the government, exercise of power or monitoring decision-makers for evidence-based decisions, potentially with biased results.

Besides, we employed principal component factor analysis to examine the latent relationships among 15 values (see Table 3.3). Since people's perceptions of what may be more or less important in the development and implementation of AI solutions can be relatively complex, abstract and difficult to articulate, it may not always be possible to capture this complexity with single questions and value items. For this reason, typological analysis offers a robust alternative and a powerful tool, as it allows for uncovering broader hidden dimensions through correlations among these individual value attributes. These dimensions can be crucial in the context of implementing ADM, AI and other data solutions in the welfare sector. For this reason, typological analysis offers a robust alternative and a powerful tool, as it allows to reveal of broader hidden dimensions through correlations among these individual value attributes. These dimensions can be crucial in the context of implementing ADM and data solutions in the welfare sector. The grouped individual value attributes form new variables or, in a sense, hidden dimensions that help describe, explain and compare citizens' overall perceptions regarding AI solutions.

In our case, we employed principal component factor analysis, a statistical method that allows grouping variables based on their inter-correlations. Our analysis revealed a statistically robust four-factor solution that best explains the underlying AI value orientations (see Table 3.3). Next factors of value estimates with respective names were extracted from the analysis:

- **Protection of Personal Interests:** This factor, representing the desire to protect humans, includes values such as privacy, accountability, security, explainability, autonomy, justice, equality and welfare. It constitutes the largest dimension, explaining 28% of the total variability.
- **Universal Solidarity:** Focused on general monitoring to ensure universal solidarity, this factor encompasses monitoring, interoperability, solidarity and welfare. It explains 17% of the total variability.

Table 3.3 Explanation of Artificial Intelligence Value Dimensions across Background Variables (Analysis of Variance)

		F1 Protection of Personal Interests		F2 Universal Solidarity		F3 Social Diversity and Solidarity		F4 Efficiency	
		Mean	F	Mean	F	Mean	F	Mean	F
Country	Estonia	0.311	192.892*	0.231	62.477*	−0.017	0.646	0.251	87.571*
	Germany	−0.307		−0.132		−0.002		−0.193	
	Sweden	0.148		−0.032		0.029		0.010	
Gender	Male	−0.019	1.713	−0.108	0.394	−0.180	150.359*	0.009	0.283
	Female	0.020		0.009		0.179		−0.007	
Age	18–34	−0.268	70.369*	−0.015	0.776	0.074	7.122*	−0.030	1.938
	35–49	−0.028		0.026		−0.076		0.046	
	59–75	0.219		0.030		−0.002		0.025	
Education	Basic	−0.310	55.898*	−0.002	6.501	−0.085	2.022	−0.228	44.572*
	Secondary	−0.072		−0.054		0.007		−0.085	
	Higher	0.142		0.061		0.014		0.157	
Agree with automation in labour[a]	Low	−0.039	6.382	0.077	22.968*	0.040	4.021	0.042	54.328*
	Middle	0.019		−0.042		−0.039		0.060	
	High	0.142		−0.261		−0.063		−0.477	
Agree with automation in social care[b]	Low	−0.090	49.413*	0.106	29.456*	0.018	0.803	0.115	45.586*
	Middle	−0.036		−0.049		−0.011		−0.023	
	High	0.307		−0.188		−0.029		−0.269	
Agree with automation in policing[c]	Low	−0.029	11.021*	0.139	80.217*	0.005	0.685	0.101	43.262*
	Middle	−0.012		−0.130		0.008		−0.109	
	High	0.204		−0.425		−0.051		−0.299	

Source: Masso et al. (2023), authors' calculations.
[a] Agreement with automation in labour, where automated classification of job seekers is applied
[b] Agreement with automation in social care, where automated assessment that a child is at risk in the family is applied
[c] Agreement with automation in predictive policing, where criminals are identified with facial recognition
*$p \leq 0.001$.

- **Social Diversity and Sustainability:** Centred on AI design considering social diversity and sustainability, this factor includes values related to justice, equality, sustainability, privacy, welfare and solidarity. It explains 15% of the total variability.
- **Efficiency:** Represented by a single variable, efficiency in terms of costs, time and resources, this factor explains 7% of the total variability.

These emergent factors reflect citizens' responses to normative values in AI guidelines, and they may represent fundamental human values regarding AI solutions. Our study indicates that certain values are robust across cultures, potentially explaining conflicts in values when designing and implementing AI systems. Estonia showed the highest and most homogeneous valuations, followed by Sweden and then Germany. Notable differences were observed in the values of security and accountability, with respondents from Estonia rating them the highest. While the third factor, reflecting social diversity and sustainability, was universally spread across the three countries, significant differences were observed in the first factor (protection of personal interests) and the second and fourth factors (universal solidarity and efficiency). Socio-demographic variables also played a role, with education, age and gender influencing the evaluation of specific factors. The associations with agreement on automation in different domains revealed that factor three, emphasising social diversity and sustainability, correlated with more universal values independent of specific automation fields. Factors two and four showed lower agreement with automation in certain domains, while factor one exhibited higher agreement in specific domains.

In sum, in previous studies, various human value models have emerged in response to societal changes, particularly the increasing integration of AI across sectors (see e.g. van de Poel, 2020). Our study aimed to develop a framework for assessing AI-related values with measurable items applicable to diverse populations across countries. Our findings confirm previous research indicating that people express their understandings and agreements or disagreements about publicly articulated AI-related value principles. Consistent with prior studies, we find that public values related to AI may align or conflict with ideals held by public managers or reflected in governmental policies. For example, while efficiency is prioritised in European governmental AI use cases, citizens tend to prioritise it less. Conversely, values like social engagement and justice, important to citizens, are relatively marginal in governmental AI applications. Therefore, the study provides insights into the values associated with AI across countries and demographic variables, contributing to a better understanding of potential conflicts and variations in AI value orientations.

However, as this analysis has shown, the valuation of these principles articulated in various guidelines, as well as the previously analysed assessments of trust, risk and suitability, is not straightforwardly explained by the welfare state models prevalent and utilised in the country. Nor may they solely be explained by individual differences within countries. Therefore, to elucidate these complex ways in which citizens perceive welfare automation, we present below a typology of adaptation, attitudes and expectations towards welfare automation.

Typology Based on Citizens' Attitudes towards Automation

Based on these analysed themes – trust and awareness, risk perception, and suitability regarding automated decision-making, as well as evaluations of various AI guidelines – we conducted an additional typological analysis. This analysis enables us to better generalise individuals' readiness for automated decision-making and compare the results within and across countries, including Estonia, Germany and Sweden. In creating the typology, we employed a statistical cluster analysis using the k-means method. This approach allows to analyse interrelationships and identify groups of individuals who have perceived welfare automation in various ways based on combinations thereof. We identified five clusters, which we have tentatively named according to the underlying perceptual features as follows – type 1: risk-inexperienced sceptics;

type 2: advocates of efficiency; type 3: social sceptics; type 4: welfare watchdogs/vigilant welfare defenders; and type 5: informed avant-gardists. Next, we will further explain the similarities and differences among these types across countries, socio-demographic characteristics and various domains of welfare automation.

Type 1: Risk-Inexperienced Sceptics

Type 1 represents individuals who rate risks associated with ADM as the lowest, compared to other types. However, they also place little importance on values related to protecting people's interests (security, autonomy, privacy, transparency, accountability, autonomy). Besides, this group generally provides the most negative assessments regarding the suitability, awareness and trust in automation. This group tends to include slightly more men, younger individuals (aged 18–34) and individuals with lower levels of education. This group consists primarily of families with children, who manage their monthly income successfully, albeit with some difficulties, based on their evaluations. This type is also characterised by a higher proportion of family-oriented individuals, which correlates with greater acceptance and perceived suitability of automation in family support services. However, there is less agreement on the use of automation in law enforcement and labour market sectors. This group constitutes an average of 13% of respondents across the three countries. However, it is predominantly represented in Germany (21%) and marginally in Sweden (7%) and Estonia (4%). Therefore, although risk-inexperienced sceptics are more prevalent in Germany, such cautious groups are still represented in the other two analysed countries.

Type 2: Advocates of Efficiency

Type 2 individuals exhibit strong trust in institutions such as the state, government, parliament, police, judiciary, healthcare, local government and media channels. Besides, they prioritise efficiency in ADM processes, emphasising cost and time savings among other resources. However, this group generally gives the most negative assessments regarding the suitability, awareness and trust in automation. Therefore, this group represents a segment where the further implementation of automated solutions could be crucial for maintaining a strong relationship between the state and the individual. Trust will be preserved if efficiency principles are prioritised, alongside other potential values. This group tends to include slightly more men, younger individuals (18–34) and individuals with varying levels of education. Compared to other groups, they also include relatively more residents of larger cities and have somewhat higher monthly incomes, which leads them to rate their daily well-being slightly better than others. Their economic security or its valuation in personal life also explains their appreciation for resource-saving in the development of automated solutions from the state's perspective. This group constitutes an average of 35% of the sample, with higher representation in Estonia (50%) compared to Sweden (33%) and Germany (26%).

Type 3: Social Sceptics

Type 3 individuals demonstrate high acceptance of ADM and express trust in such solutions. However, this group holds scepticism regarding the reliability of computer systems. They prioritise social values such as diversity, justice, equality and sustainability, particularly in the development and use of automated tools in public administration and the welfare sector, but prioritise these foremost in areas like automated family benefits (compared to the domains of policing and employment services, where they less agree with automation). This group tends to include slightly more women, individuals aged 50–79 and those with vocational education. This group also includes more residents from smaller cities, divorced or single individuals and single parents who rate their daily living conditions as modest or poor based on their monthly income. This group predominantly consists of residents from Germany (26%) and Sweden (22%), with significantly fewer from Estonia (9%) (averaging 20%). These differences can be attributed to Estonia's relatively 'young' state, where welfare state traditions have developed only in the last few decades, compared to Sweden and Germany.

Type 4: Welfare Watchdogs/Vigilant Welfare Defenders

Type 4 individuals demonstrate a strong commitment to monitoring (controlling the automation process), solidarity (inclusion of people, social cohesion) and welfare (benefits for individuals). They strongly criticise automation that solely prioritises efficiency (cost, time and other resource savings). They also perceive potential risks and dangers associated with automation relatively more often than others. However, they maintain moderate trust in national institutions. This group tends to include slightly more men, in Estonia, and also more Russian speakers. In terms of other characteristics such as place of residence, income and education, this group does not stand out, indicating a relatively equal distribution across these attributes. This group constitutes 12% in general, being somewhat more spread in Germany (16%), compared to Sweden (7%) and Estonia (9%). Therefore, although efficiency is often the primary argument for developing automated solutions from both public and governmental perspectives, this group represents a small yet vocal and significant demographic that criticises developments based solely on efficiency without considering monitoring and social values.

Type 5: Informed Avant-gardists

Individuals in this group are the most informed about ADM (e.g. the right to demand that decisions affecting them as data providers be made by humans; the right as data providers to demand an explanation of how decisions were reached, etc.). However, they also exhibit significantly higher trust in automated decisions compared to other types, although they assess potential risks and dangers more critically and express somewhat more modest trust in institutions compared to other clusters. Therefore, they emphasise the importance of addressing technical risks (security, transparency, privacy, explainability) in the development of automated solutions. This group tends to include more women, individuals aged 35–49, slightly more Russian speakers in Estonia and highly educated individuals. This group predominantly consists of residents of smaller towns and rural areas, single individuals and those with below-average incomes who therefore rate their economic well-being as modest. Interestingly, a connection with religion emerged: while they do not consider themselves overtly religious, they do follow certain religious traditions, such as frequently attending places of worship. This group constitutes nearly one-fifth of the respondents on average (20%). While Swedish and Estonian residents are relatively equally represented in this group, at 31% and 29%, respectively, it is significantly smaller among German respondents, at 16%. Therefore, this group may view ADM and other technological solutions as a new source of faith, from which they hope to improve their living conditions.

The typological analysis revealed that, in addition to identifying specific characteristics of automated decision-making highlighted in the previous analysis of individual traits, where we classified individuals as 'informed sceptics' (Germany), 'wild natives' (Estonia), and 'agreeing conformists' (Sweden), significant differences also exist between countries and welfare contexts. Considering the varying levels of readiness among individuals, as indicated by the typological analysis, is crucial for understanding the diversity of citizens' attitudes towards the implementation of automated solutions. This understanding also helps explain the reasons behind potential frictions and failures in implementing digital care when applying data-based, automated, and AI-driven systems.

Conclusions

This chapter engaged with the experiences, perceptions and attitudes towards ADM of citizens in Estonia, Germany and Sweden based on a population-representative, comparative survey in the three countries. We relate these specific perceptions of ADM – that include awareness, trust and risk perception – to societal trust and find that there are important differences between the three countries. Initially, we observed certain country-specific patterns in trust, risk perception and suitability evaluations of ADM – provisionally labelling these welfare types as 'the wild natives of ADM' (example of Estonia), 'informed sceptics' (example of Germany) and 'agreeing conformists' (example of Sweden).

Our study highlighted the intricate dynamics of technological innovation of the data welfare state across Sweden, Germany and Estonia. Swedes are cautious about adopting ADM while maintaining strong trust in social institutions, reflecting their confidence in civil servants within a robust social democratic welfare framework. Germans similarly approach ADM with scepticism, driven by lower overall social trust and a corporate– statist welfare orientation less focused on distributive justice. In contrast, Estonia shows significant enthusiasm for ADM despite lower social trust, driven by rapid social changes and a national identity intertwined with digital advancements. This suggests that ADM in Estonia could enhance trust in public administration aligned with values of fairness and justice. The study emphasises the need to contextualise citizen attitudes within diverse welfare state frameworks and calls for tailored implementations of EU regulations like the GDPR to accommodate regional differences in public perceptions and expectations regarding ADM.

A closer analysis, however, revealed significant differences *within* the welfare models of each country. The developed typology, using statistical cluster analysis and analysing the associations between the aggregated index variables across thematic areas – trust, risk perception, suitability assessment and values, enabled us to identify of groups whose perceptions of welfare automation varied based on these combinations. We categorised these groups into five clusters: type 1: risk-inexperienced sceptics; type 2: advocates of efficiency; type 3: social sceptics; type 4: welfare watchdogs/vigilant welfare defenders; and type 5: informed avant-gardists. Each type exhibited distinct characteristics across countries, socio-demographic profiles and domains of welfare automation, revealing nuanced differences within each national welfare model.

References

Araujo, T., Helberger, N., Kruikemeier, S., & De Vreese, C. H. (2020). In AI we trust? Perceptions about automated decision-making by artificial intelligence. *AI & Society*, 35, 611–623.

Binns, R. (2018). What can political philosophy teach us about algorithmic fairness? *IEEE Security & Privacy*, 16(3), 73–80, https://doi.org/10.1109/MSP.2018.2701147

Borgesius, F. J. Z. (2020). Strengthening legal protection against discrimination by algorithms and artificial intelligence. *International Journal of Human Rights*, 24(10), 1572–1593. https://doi.org/10.1080/13642987.2020.1743976

Brown, A., Chouldechova, A., Putnam-Hornstein, E., Tobin, A., & Vaithianathan, R. (2019). Toward algorithmic accountability in public services: A qualitative study of affected community perspectives on algorithmic decision-making in child welfare services. In *Proceedings of the 2019 CHI Conference on Human Factors in Computing Systems* (pp. 1–12). ACM Digital Library. https://doi.org/10.1145/3290605.3300271

Dencik, L., Hintz, A., & Carey, Z. (2018). Prediction, pre-emption and limits to dissent: Social media and big data uses for policing protests in the United Kingdom. *New Media & Society*, 20(4), 1433–1450. https://doi.org/10.1177/1461444817697722

Eklund, L., Stamm, I., & Liebermann, W. K. (2019). The crowd in crowdsourcing: Crowdsourcing as a pragmatic research method. *First Monday*, 24(10). https://doi.org/10.5210/fm.v24i10.9206

Eubanks, V. (2018). *Automating inequality: How high-tech tools profile, police, and punish the poor* (First ed.). St. Martin's Press.

Fatima, S., Desouza, K. C., Buck, C., & Fielt, E. (2022). Public AI canvas for AI-enabled public value: A design science approach. *Government Information Quarterly*, *39*(4), 101722. https://doi.org/10.1016/j.giq.2022.101722

General Data Protection Regulation (EU) 2016/679. (2016). *In Regulation (EU) 2016/679 of the European Parliament and of the Council of 27 April 2016 on the protection of natural persons with regard to the processing of personal data and on the free movement of such data, and repealing Directive 95/46/EC* (General Data Protection Regulation). https://eur-lex.europa.eu/eli/reg/2016/679/oj

Gesk, T. S., & Leyer, M. (2022). Artificial intelligence in public services: When and why citizens accept its usage. *Government Information Quarterly*, *39*(3), 101704. https://doi.org/10.1016/j.giq.2022.101704

Hagendorff, T. (2020). The ethics of AI ethics: An evaluation of guidelines. *Minds and Machines*, *30*(1), 99–120. https://doi.org/10.1007/s11023-020-09517-8

Han, S., Kelly, E., Nikou, S., & Svee, E.-O. (2022). Aligning artificial intelligence with human values: Reflections from a phenomenological perspective. *AI & Society*, *37*(4), 1383–1395. https://doi.org/10.1007/s00146-021-01247-4

Helberger, N., Araujo, T., & de Vreese, C. H. (2020). Who is the fairest of them all? Public attitudes and expectations regarding automated decision-making. *Computer Law & Security Report*, *39*, 105456. https://doi.org/10.1016/j.clsr.2020.105456

Henriksen, A., & Blond, L. (2023). Executive-centered AI? Designing predictive systems for the public sector. *Social Studies of Science*. https://doi.org/10.1177/03063127231163756

Hockenhull, M., & Cohn, M. L. (2021). Hot air and corporate sociotechnical imaginaries: Performing and translating digital futures in the Danish tech scene. *New Media & Society*, *23*(2), 302–321. https://doi.org/10.1177/1461444820929319

Ingrams, A., Kaufmann, W., & Jacobs, D. (2022). In AI we trust? Citizen perceptions of AI in government decision making. *Policy & Internet*, *14*(2), 390–409. https://doi.org/10.1002/poi3.276

Jørgensen, R. F., & Søe, S. O. (2023). Metaphors at work: Reconciling welfare and market in Danish digitalisation policies. *Media, Culture & Society*. https://doi.org/10.1177/01634437231188463

König, P. D., Wurster, S., & Siewert, M. B. (2022). Consumers are willing to pay a price for explainable, but not for green AI. Evidence from a choice-based conjoint analysis. *Big Data & Society*, *9*(1). https://doi.org/10.1177/20539517211069632

Kalmus, V., Lauristin, M., Opermann, S., & Vihalemm, T. (2020). *Researching Estonian transformation: Morphogenetic reflections*. Tartu University Press.

Kasapoglu, T., & Masso, A. (2021). Attaining security through algorithms: Perspectives of refugees and data experts. In J. B. Wiest (Ed.), *Theorizing criminality and policing in the digital media age* (pp. 47–65). Emerald Publishing. (Studies in Media and Communications)

Kasapoglu, T., Masso, A., & Calzati, S. (2021). Unpacking algorithms as technologies of power: Syrian refugees and data experts on algorithmic governance. *Digital Geography and Society*, *2*, 100016. https://doi.org/10.1016/j.diggeo.2021.100016

Kasirzadeh, A., & Gabriel, I.. (2022). In conversation with Artificial Intelligence: Aligning language models with human values. *arXiv*. https://doi.org/10.48550/arXiv.2209.00731

Kaun, A., Larsson, A. O., & Masso, A. (2023). Automating public administration: Citizens' attitudes towards automated decision-making across Estonia, Sweden, and Germany. *Information, Communication & Society 27*2, 314–332. https://doi.org/10.1080/1369118X.2023.2205493

Larsson, S. (2020). On the governance of artificial intelligence through ethics guidelines. *Asian Journal of Law and Society, 7*(3), 437–451.

Lomborg, S., Kaun, A., & Scott Hansen, S. (2023). Automated decision-making: Toward a people-centred approach. *Sociology Compass*, e13097.

Männiste, M., & Masso, A. (2018). The role of institutional trust in Estonians' privacy concerns. *Studies of Transition States and Societies, 10*(2).

Masso, A., & Kasapoglu, T. (2020). Understanding power positions in a new digital landscape: Perceptions of Syrian refugees and data experts on relocation algorithm. *Information, Communication & Society, 23*(8), 1203–1219. https://doi.org/10.1080/1369118X.2020.1739731

Masso, A., Kaun, A., & van Noordt, C. (2023). Basic values in artificial intelligence: Comparative factor analysis in Estonia, Germany, and Sweden. *AI & Society*. https://doi.org/10.1007/s00146-023-01750-w

Ranerup, A., & Svensson, L. (2023). Automated decision-making, discretion and public values: A case study of two municipalities and their case management of social assistance. *European Journal of Social Work*, 1–15.

Reutter, L. (2022). Constraining context: Situating datafication in public administration. *New Media & Society, 24*(4), 903–921. https://doi.org/10.1177/14614448221079029

Schlüter, E., Masso, A., & Davidov, E. (2019). What factors explain anti-muslim prejudice? A comparative assessment of Muslim population size, institutional characteristics and immigration-related media claims. *Journal of Ethnic and Migration Studies*, 1–16.

Schmidt, J.-H., & Weichert, T. (2012). *Datenschutz: Grundlagen, Entwicklungen und Kontroversen: Vol. Band 1190*. bpb, Bundeszentrale für Politische Bildung.

Strümke, I., Slavkovik, M., & Madai, V. I. (2021). The social dilemma in artificial intelligence development and why we have to solve it. *AI and Ethics*. https://doi.org/10.1007/s43681-021-00120-w

Szolnoki, G., & Hoffmann, D. (2013). Online, face-to-face and telephone surveys—comparing different sampling methods in wine consumer research. *Wine Economics and Policy, 2*(2), 57–66. https://doi.org/10.1016/j.wep.2013.10.001

Umbrello, S. (2022). The role of engineers in harmonising human values for AI systems design. *Journal of Responsible Technology, 10*, 100031. https://doi.org/10.1016/j.jrt.2022.100031

van de Poel, I. (2020). Embedding values in artificial intelligence (AI) systems. *Minds and Machines, 30*(3), 385–409. https://doi.org/10.1007/s11023-020-09537-4

Veale, M., & Edwards, L. (2018). Clarity, surprises, and further questions in the Article 29 Working Party draft guidance on automated decision-making and profiling. *Computer Law & Security Report, 34*(2), 398–404.

Vihalemm, P., Masso, A., & Opermann, S. (2017). *The Routledge international handbook of European social transformations*. Routledge.

Wagner, W., Viidalepp, A., Idoiaga-Mondragon, N., Talves, K., Lillemäe, E., Pekarev, J., & Otsus, M. (2023). Lay representations of artificial intelligence and autonomous military machines. *Public Understanding of Science*, *32*(7), 926–943. https://doi.org/10.1177/09636625231167071

Wang, B. (2022). *Public value and social development*. Springer Nature.

Wirtz, B. W., & Müller, W. M. (2019). An integrated artificial intelligence framework for public management. *Public Management Review*, *21*(7), 1076–1100.

Wu, D. (2023). Good for tech: Disability expertise and labor in China's artificial intelligence sector. *First Monday*.

Züger, T., & Asghari, H. (2022). AI for the public. How public interest theory shifts the discourse on AI. *AI & SOCIETY*. https://doi.org/10.1007/s00146-022-01480-5

4
(Re-)Configuring Data Welfare

Scene: A false accusation and the impact of automated detection. The year is 2021 and Erik is woken up by police forces storming his apartment. The first question they ask is where his laptop is. Erik is arrested, not understanding what for. When he realises that he is accused of owning and distributing child pornography, he is in shock. It later turned out that pictures sent between him and his boyfriend, which were not even very delicate or sensitive, were highlighted automatically by a child pornography detection software in the United States. The US officials reported the findings back to the Swedish police who reacted swiftly. After the investigation and all charges being dropped, Erik wondered if he should be compensated for the harm that was done to him and also how he could contribute to preventing others from being exposed to similar experiences in the future. In a first step, a larger journalistic investigation was initiated.

Influencing and reconfiguring largely invisible infrastructures of control is difficult if not impossible for individual citizens and civil society organisations. How do we relate to and negotiate technological black boxes that are often presented as complex and hard to explain to lay persons? How do we exercise agency and participate in the future formation of such systems? This chapter explores forms of citizen engagement to influence the outset of the data welfare state. This refers to work by journalists, citizens and advocacy groups as well as unions who actively engage in the discussions around the advantages and the dark side of the data welfare state. The effort of these groups is very much focused on establishing the data welfare state as a political rather than a merely administrative issue. Based on the discussion of several cases of citizen engagement around the data welfare state, this chapter develops ways ahead for the data welfare state discussing aspirations and potential alternative futures that move beyond the emphasis of efficiency. The chapter also pushes the boundaries of early critiques of data welfare and presents answers to the question 'what can be done' beyond values of transparency and accountability. Ultimately the chapter reinforces the assumption that data welfare is fundamentally about how we want to live our lives together in societies that allow for human flourishing and prosperity.

There is a growing body of literature within critical data studies that engages with forms of resistance and agency in the light of injustices that emerge in algorithmic culture.

For example, Tiziano Bonini and Emiliano Treré explore different forms of resistance against algorithms, highlighting small acts of non-compliance by gig workers, creative practices to resist algorithms in cultural production and lastly algorithmic resistance in relation to political practices. Similar to Chapter 2 in this book, the focus is on everyday and mundane practices and forms of engagement with and around algorithms as an expression of agency. In relation to algorithmic agency, Nick Couldry (2024) conceptualises the four ways in which social movements have been datafied. First, datafication is a broader background against which social movements are evolving. Second, data have become a *specific* object of contestation, namely social movements are criticising how individuals are represented in databases or excluded from them as well as how different databases are combined and, in that way, provide a tightening network of data points and representations of private individuals. Third, data have become a *general* object of contestation by social movements. Here, Couldry refers to critique and resistance against data infrastructures such as big tech. Fourth, data have become intrinsic to social movements' methods and practices of resistance. Our conceptualisation of the double movement of datafication that we develop in Chapter 1 is similar to Couldry's approach. While social movements are increasingly datafied, they also develop important critiques and hence contribute to potential changes in how datafication takes shape. This double nature or what Hepp and Görland (2024) call a relational approach to datafication is central to our arguments on the data welfare state and especially when it comes to ways of negotiating its shape that are at the heart of this chapter.

While the focus of Bonini and Treré's (2024) exploration is on individuals and cultural practices, we are here interested in forms of critique and resistance that are highlighted by organisations and groups and directly targeting the bureaucratic welfare state. These perspectives receive a heightened urgency in the context of the data welfare state as citizens and persons within a certain state regime hardly can opt out data infrastructures of the state. In contrast to much other previous research, we are highlighting expressions of support and acceptance of the data welfare state, while not buying into the utopian, grandiose narratives of the smartification of the state.

One major point of discussion is in how far the bureaucratic state apparatus ever was exposed or thought of in terms of participation by the people in its confines. The bureaucratic apparatus has been and is considered largely as a black box (Carlsson, 2023; Dubois, 2016; Jarvis, 2014). The policy discussions here focus mainly on questions of accountability and transparency to open up the bureaucratic black box for scrutiny and civic participation. Consequently, with the datafication of the welfare state, similar arguments emerged while adding a layer of technological fuzziness to the existing black box problem.

The black box problem has been acknowledged on the policy level regulating automated decision-making (ADM) in the General Data Protection Regulation to render it more transparent. Accordingly, persons have the right to 'human' decisions and being informed whether a decision has been automated or not. Following-up on job seekers in the Swedish context and their exposure to automated systems as discussed in Chapter 2, we today know very little about the extent to which people make use of these rights. There are currently no statistics available about complaints or objections towards automated decisions within the Swedish Employment Services.

We organise this chapter around practices of negotiation that encompass small mundane acts of, for example, finding ways to adjust to requirements set by automated system to critical perceptions of certain forms of automation that are expressed in civic talk and also more structured and organised forms of trying to make opaque systems transparent (i.e. through mapping initiatives) and testing legal grounds through litigation. To depict individuals' encounters with ADM, we showcase personal narratives from two domains: labour market offices and the police. These instances vividly demonstrate that people are invested in decisions and automated solutions that shape their experiences, significantly influencing their daily lives.

Mapping and Counter-Mapping as Methods to Critically Engage With the Data Welfare State

In order to allow for civic participation around the data welfare state to happen, there is a need for information on data-based practices and ADM systems in use. One important way to allow for increased visibility that fosters civic talk about the data welfare state is mapping and counter-mapping initiatives. Already in 2018, Joanna Redden (2018) employed counter-mapping as a way to engage with big data practices of the Canadian state, identifying modes of justification as well as challenges in the implementation of big data analytics in the public sector. Redden identifies in the materials gathered for the counter-mapping benefits and promises as well as risks and challenges in engaging big data analytics in the public sector. This initiative has now been transformed and expanded to a database of automated systems used by the Canadian public services.

Besides the work by the data justice lab, there are a number of initiatives trying to map the extent of artificial intelligence (AI) and ADM applications in the public sector. Generally, we can distinguish between top-down and bottom-up initiatives. While top-down initiatives refer to mapping attempts initiated by policy makers and regulators, bottom-up initiatives are steered rather by grassroot initiatives. A prominent example in the top-down category is the registries developed by Finnish company Saidot that developed accessible platforms gathering algorithms used in the cities of Helsinki and Amsterdam. Based on reports by city employees, the platforms provide information on ADM systems in use relating to purpose and impact, accountability, datasets, data processing, issues of discrimination, oversight, risks and mitigation as well as explainability (Trifuljesko, 2022). According to Sonja Trifuljesko (2022), the registries were developed in order to enact meaningful transparency while not being particularly clear for whom and to what ends. Similarly, the European Commission's Joint Research Centre AI Watch has developed a database to map the 'European landscape on the use of artificial intelligence by the public sector' (Joint Research Centre at the European Commission, 2022). Last updated in 2021, the database currently includes 686 cases across all European countries (European Commission Joint Research Centre (JRC), 2021). In addition, some national agencies provide listings of projects underway, for instance, if they receive public funding. This is the case for the Danish so-called 'Signatur-projekter' with AI in municipalities and regional government bodies, projects which are publicly declared and formally backed by the Danish Agency for Digitalisation.

More bottom-up initiatives include mapping initiatives conducted by NGOs and civic groups such as AlgorithmWatch that has released several reports on the use of ADM generally and in the public sector more specifically (AlgorithmWatch, 2019, 2020). Another case in point is the Data Harms Project conducted by the Data Justice Lab based at Cardiff University that aimed at documenting harm caused by algorithmic systems (Redden, 2018). The lab also worked on mapping cancelled ADM systems in the public sector globally, taking the cancelation as an indicator that civic initiatives sometimes lobby successfully against the implementation or upscaling of specific and problematic ADM systems (Redden et al., 2022). In the Swedish context, Lupita Svensson (2019) conducted a study of all 290 municipalities and the degree of ADM in their work. The report was initiated by the union SSR that represents among others civil servants and social workers. There are also numerous research initiatives that both map and report on the development of AI in the public and welfare sector including the Stanford University's Human-Centered Artificial Intelligence Centre that publishes the Artificial Intelligence Index (2024).

Investigating and Questioning the Data Welfare State Through Litigation

Besides mapping ADM and AI systems in the public sector, there have been attempts to open the algorithmic black box through litigation. Part of the engagement is legal definitions of public records and freedom of information when it comes to algorithms. In the Swedish context, access to public records is one of the core values to undergird the democratic system. With the implementation of algorithmic systems for decision-making, the question emerged whether algorithms should count as public records and hence fall under the legal framework of access to public records. The question was tested famously by a journalist starting a litigation case against Trelleborg municipality and its fully automated system for decisions on social benefits (see Chapter 2). As part of a general discussion on how welfare provision is changing with digitalisation and in particular algorithm-based decision-making (Alston, 2019; Kaun, 2022), several actors started to explore the so-called Trelleborg model further that we have introduced in Chapter 2. Firstly, the journalist Fredrik Ramel engaged in the discussion about transparency of the ADM system used in Trelleborg. After several failed attempts to get access to the source code from Trelleborg municipality and reaching out to the Danish company that was responsible for the coding, he took legal steps: He submitted an appeal to an Administrative Court of Appeal arguing that the source code of the software used falls under the Swedish principle of public access to official records (*Offentlighetsprincipen*). The court followed his appeal and ruled that the source code has to be made accessible to the public and is fully included in the principle of public access (Dagenssamhälle, 2020).

After the ruling of the Administrative Court was made public, another group of journalists at the newspaper *Dagenssamhälle* submitted a Freedom of Information Request in accordance with the principle of public access to official records to gain access to the source code. Trelleborg municipality forwarded the request to the Danish software company who delivered the code that was in turn shared with the journalists. The material was, however, not submitted to a security check and sensitive data including personal numbers (comparable to social security number), names and information about elderly care at home were delivered to the journalists (Dagenssamhälle, 2020).

A second case of testing the access to 'meaningful information' on algorithmic decision-making involved the Union for Professionals (*Akademikerförbundet SSR*) in Sweden that is related to the Trelleborg case that we also discuss in Chapter 2 of this book. In 2018, Simon Vinge, chief economist at the Union for Professionals, reported the municipality of Trelleborg to the Parliamentary Ombudsman (PO) (*Justitieombudsmannen JO*). He complained about the fact that the authorities failed to respond to a Freedom of Information Request related to robotic process automation use to deliver automated decisions.

The trade union SSR did not request access to the source code of the software for automated decisions but requested 'meaningful information' on how decisions are made with the help of the algorithmic system. In the process that started in June 2018, he had several conversations and meetings with representatives from Trelleborg municipality to discuss what meaningful information in relation to the algorithmic system might mean. He was shown a short film that explained the process of automation and reached the conclusion that he would like to receive screenshots of the programme interface that is used by the civil servants for processing and administering social benefit applications. After waiting for almost a year without hearing back, he reported Trelleborg municipality to the PO for delaying the response and the inability to provide meaningful information on how decisions are made with the help of the algorithm-based system. The report to the PO is based on a formulation in the State Public Report 'Jurisprudence for the support of the digitalization of public administration' from 2018 (SOU, 2018, p. 25) that emphasises the right to 'meaningful information on the logics behind as well as the expected consequences' of automation for the individual person.

The main argument is that the democratic rights of individual citizens are constrained if meaningful information about how automated decisions are executed are missing. The union furthermore argued that meaningful information has to be accessible to and comprehensible for lay people without programming knowledge. According to the union, the municipality is lacking routines and definitions of what meaningful information encompasses in the case of automated decisions on social benefit applications. In an opinion piece published in *Svenska Dagbladet*, Simon Vinge and Heike Erkers (chair of the Union for Professionals) (2020-01-18) argue further that the delegation of decisions is not regulated in the delegation system of the municipality and hence the algorithm – or in their words robot – acts illegally. In 2021, the PO reacted and supported the complaints by SSR. The union continued to engage in discussions around algorithmic governance (Akademikerförbundet SSR, 2024) and for example proposed the implementation of an Algorithm Ombudsman as public agency that provides oversight of algorithmic automation in the public sector (Akademikerförbund SSR, 2020).

Exploring Data Welfare State Through Future Scenarios

Besides the engagement by journalists and unions as representatives in the public sphere, we sought to understand citizens' resisting and promoting data welfare state. In order to make the engagement of citizens with ADM possible, we developed a scenario-based approach presented in the quantitative survey. These scenarios illustrate the impact of the data welfare state, which increasingly relies on algorithmic tools for decision-making. These scenarios were crafted to mirror established discussions on ADM systems in the public sector. However, it is important to note that the specific figures for failure rates and the models used for risk scores in these scenarios are entirely fictional and are not explicitly tied to any national context. Instead, the intention was to present realistic scenarios without delving into specific and potentially contentious cases of ADM in practice.

We employed a scenario-based approach to study citizens' reflections on the potential outcomes resulting from the implementation of ADM. More in detail, our study examined three ADM scenarios: employment services, child welfare prediction and predictive policing (Figure 4.1) (Kaun et al., 2023). Our results revealed that in general, German respondents prefer ADM in employment services, Swedes prioritise child welfare and Estonians support predictive policing. However, significant variations in perceptions of ADM efficiency and fairness exist among the countries. In employment services, Germans view ADM more positively than Swedes and Estonians. Swedes favour ADM in child welfare, while Estonians prefer facial recognition for crime prevention. The study highlights unique national attitudes towards the applications of ADM in different contexts, which will be elaborated further in the following sections (see also Kaun et al., 2023).

The first scenario we included into our study involves ADM in unemployment services, automating job chance evaluations based on a 20-item questionnaire. Job seekers are categorised and provided tailored training and support. This is referred to as the employment services scenario. The second scenario predicts child welfare, assigning risk scores based on family background and housing situations. Termed the social services scenario, it triggers specific remedies such as home visits. The third scenario focuses on predictive policing with facial recognition, automatically stopping and questioning individuals triggering hits in the database, despite a higher false positive rate. Referred to as the predictive policing scenario, respondents' perceptions of system deployment are explored.

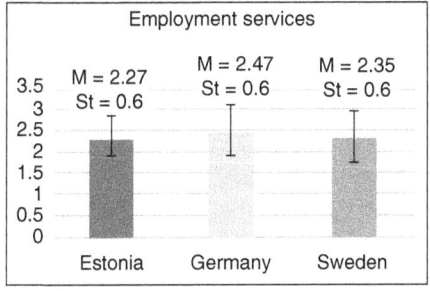
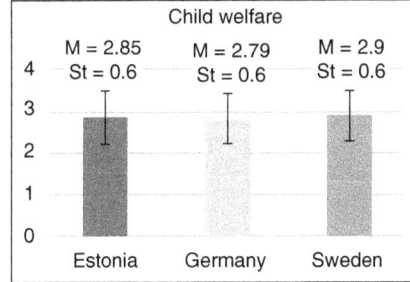
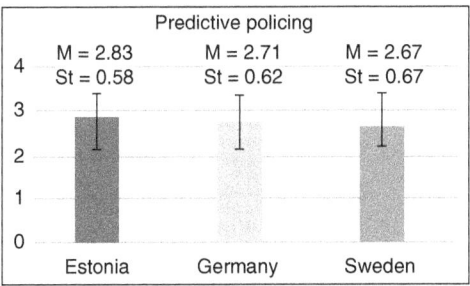

Figure 4.1 Scenario Index on the Attitudes Towards Automated Decision-Making Across Domains (Mean and Standard Deviation, Higher Value Indicates More Positive Attitude)
Source: Authors' Figure based on Kaun, Larsson, Masso, 2024.

The findings reveal that German respondents perceive ADM in employment services as more efficient, objective and just compared to their Estonian and Swedish counterparts. In the employment services scenario, Germans showed a more positive outlook (m = 2.47) compared to Swedes (m = 2.35) and Estonians (m = 2.27). Notably, the variations across mean values were relatively consistent in all cases (standard deviation approximately around 0.6).

Regarding child welfare, Swedish respondents view ADM as beneficial for preventing harm, efficient and more just. Specifically, in the social services scenario, Swedish respondents exhibited the highest positivity (m = 2.9) towards the child welfare scenario. Estonian respondents were somewhat less enthusiastic (m = 2.85), and German respondents expressed limited agreement on average (m = 2.79). However, similar to estimates for employment services, variations around the mean were relatively low and comparable across countries.

Finally, regarding the use of facial recognition for crime prevention, Estonian respondents perceive it as more efficient, objective and less concerning regarding false accusations. In our predictive policing scenario, Estonian respondents demonstrated greater positivity (m = 2.83) compared to their German (m = 2.71) and Swedish (m = 2.67) counterparts. However, the variation around the mean value, measured by standard deviation, was lowest in Estonia ($\sigma = 0.58$), in contrast to Germany ($\sigma = 0.62$) and Sweden ($\sigma = 0.67$).

This indicates that despite the overall positive evaluations in Estonia, there is still a considerable number with both very positive and negative estimates.

Furthermore, we conducted an examination of how independent variables explain the results revealed by the scenario indices. The results indicated, that gender did not show significant effects, whereas age consistently emerged as a positive predictor across all countries, indicating that older respondents tend to view employment services more positively. Conversely, education demonstrated a significant negative impact, suggesting that higher levels of education are associated with greater scepticism. Awareness of citizen rights concerning ADM did not notably affect the scenario index for employment services. However, the trust index, reflecting respondents' trust in societal actors, emerged as a significant negative predictor in Germany and Estonia, indicating that higher institutional trust is linked to more scepticism towards automation in the field employment services.

Although gender does not significantly predict attitudes towards the employment services scenario, it yielded negative and significant coefficients for the social services scenario, particularly in Germany and Estonia. This suggests that male respondents are less positive about the social services scenario compared to their female counterparts. Age, showed significant estimates across all countries, indicating older respondents are more positive towards both social services and employment services scenarios. The education variable did not reach significance. In contrast, the awareness index, behaving similarly for employment services, showed a different result for social services. It emerged as negative and significant (for Germany and Estonia), indicating that higher awareness about rights related to ADM correlates with more negative attitudes towards the social services scenario. Respondents enthusiastic about ADM tend to be more positive, while those with higher trust in societal institutions are less enthusiastic about the scenario.

While age consistently appeared as a positive significant explanatory variable in the previous scenarios, its role in predicting attitudes towards predictive policing differed. In Estonia and Sweden, older respondents displayed more scepticism towards predictive policing. Unlike the education variable's negative impact on the employment services scenario, higher education had a positive effect on attitudes towards predictive policing across all countries, reaching significance in Germany and Sweden. Higher education levels were associated with more positive views on predictive policing. The awareness index had a negative impact across all countries, significantly so for Sweden, indicating that higher awareness led to decreased scenario index scores in all three scenarios. The two remaining variables, finding ADM suitable and expressing trust in societal institutions, behaved consistently, with finding ADM suitable leading to higher scenario index scores and expressing trust in institutions leading to lower scenario index scores. Positive coefficients indicated that as the independent variable increased, the mean of the dependent variable tended to increase, while negative coefficients suggested a decrease in the dependent variable as the independent variable increased.

Therefore, the results revealed that each analysed country exhibits a preference for a specific ADM scenario – Germany for job seeker categorisation, Sweden for social services and Estonia for predictive policing. This underscores significant domain-specific variations in citizens' evaluations of ADM across welfare regimes. Germans display greater positivity towards employment services automation, reflecting a job market–focused welfare setting. Swedes prioritise child welfare, aligning with their strong social welfare traditions. Estonians favour predictive policing, indicative of their emphasis on crime prevention and technology's role in nation branding. These distinctions highlight the influence of specific welfare contexts on citizens' attitudes towards ADM applications.

How can we make sense of these differences? In Germany, there is a longer tradition of public discourse on implementing digital solutions in the public sector (Schmidt & Weichert, 2012). Additionally, the corporatist–statist welfare regime in Germany focuses less on distributive logics compared to the social democratic regime. Citizens may perceive ADM primarily as a tool for controlling and surveilling welfare distribution rather than providing care. This focus on surveillance and control is reflected in their stronger preference for less invasive scenarios, such as the job seeker scenario. In contrast, Swedish respondents may prefer the social service scenario due to the historically strong position of children's rights in Sweden. Sweden's social democratic welfare regime, with its expansive welfare institutions including trusted social services, likely contributes to this preference.

Estonians show considerable enthusiasm for ADM, particularly in the context of predictive policing. This positive attitude may be attributed to Estonia's supportive general stance towards ADM and predictive policing, influenced by the prominent role of algorithmic systems in public administration and digital technologies within the country (Männiste & Masso, 2020; Tammpuu & Masso, 2018). These findings suggest that ADM technology has the potential to foster renewed trust in public administration among Estonians, connecting with values of fairness and justice embedded in technology. This trust is especially crucial in the context of crime and punishment. Moreover, ADM may contribute to shaping perceptions of crime, security and safety, participating in the formation of social norms and values related to security in Estonia.

Gender, age, education and trust play distinct roles in shaping attitudes towards ADM scenarios. Gender is a significant factor, particularly for the social services scenario, where male respondents are more sceptical than their female counterparts. This scepticism might stem from the traditional caregiving role often held by women, making them more open to ADM's potential in identifying families in need of support.

Generally, age is a noteworthy factor, with higher age generally correlating with more positive attitudes across scenarios, except for predictive policing. In this case, older respondents tend to be more negative, suggesting a shift in the age effect when faced with a more uncertain and intrusive scenario. The changing meanings of police work over time might be reflected in the varying attitudes across generations. On the other hand, education has diverging effects on different scenarios. For employment and social service scenarios, higher education leads to more negative attitudes. Highly educated respondents disagree with the suitability of these scenarios. However, for predictive policing, higher education becomes a positive predictor, indicating that more educated individuals, potentially with higher digital skills, see less risk of wrongful examination by the police. This suggests that attitudes towards predictive policing may reveal class-based differences among respondents.

Besides, trust consistently influences attitudes across scenarios and welfare regimes. The more trust respondents express for societal institutions, the more negative they are towards ADM scenarios. This highlights the importance of trust as a cross-cutting factor shaping attitudes in various domains and welfare settings.

In conclusion, our survey results highlight significant differences related to welfare regimes and specific domains of ADM deployment. Governing and regulating ADM applications based on citizens' preferences must consider these variations. Citizens differentiate between ADM technologies and their application areas, and these distinctions are influenced by both the welfare regime context and individual factors such as age, gender, education and societal trust. Therefore, understanding attitudes towards ADM in digital welfare research requires a holistic consideration of both individual and structural factors, emphasising the necessity for domain-specific approaches to ADM governance.

Controversial Interactions With Public Agencies: Experiences of Long-Term Unemployed

Beyond the measurement of attitudes towards scenarios of ADM that are expression of how citizens negotiate the data welfare state, we aimed at in-depth explorations of experiences with the data welfare state and conducted in-depth interviews with long-term unemployed and job seekers more generally. Job seekers as a group of citizens who are more likely to have frequent interactions with public agencies have expressed particular experiences and understandings of what is changing with data-based technologies in the welfare sector. In interviews that we conducted with long-time unemployed in Sweden in 2022, respondents often link their individual experiences to overall changes in public administration and in particular with the employment services. In our interviews with long-term unemployed, we used current AI-related projects by the employment services such as the automation case detailed in Chapter 2 as prompts. After the description of a pilot project aimed at matching job seekers automatically with suitable job openings after an automated analysis of job descriptions with the help of a language model, this respondent, for example, replied:

> It's more like a question of how and if the Employment Services work at all today. I do not know what they gain from this [comment by authors: data-based automation] more than showing off some kind of more fine-grained statistics. It's how I perceive the Employment Services more generally, like they do a lot of analyses and pilots but they lead nowhere. (long-term unemployed in their 50s)

The AI and data-based projects are seen in the broader context of reforming the employment services and the general perception of their work rather than isolated projects. It is the overall perception of the public agency that is of importance to the respondent. However, the projects gain the role of standing in for generally approaching large, structural projects with quick fixes that often divert energy and resources, but not necessarily revolve fundamental challenges. Another aspect that is mentioned is the perception of job seekers by the agency that is partly reflected in how their needs are met with standardised responses. The respondent argues:

> And this is connected to my experience that all job seekers are considered as one big gray mass (...). You get into these different programmes and everyone is just treated the same, there is no possibility to get into a programme that is maybe a bit more specialized (...). (long-term unemployed in their 50s from Sweden)

During the interviews, a disconnect also emerged between the data and information available to automated system profiling job seekers. There are aspects such as educational certificates that might indicate a certain level of knowledge or interest but that have little to do with actual work experiences as this interviewee as well in their 50s and from a mid-sized Swedish city expresses:

> This [automated matching of job seekers and job openings] is super interesting. It reminds me of, how do you say it, the expression, looks good on paper. Because these are people who have other things then it might say in their CVs, like I have credits and a degree in like humanities, which is totally irrelevant for my job. [...] I guess it would be good with some kind of automated foundation, but then a person needs to take over and dig deeper. (long-term unemployed in their 50s from Sweden)

While many of our respondents first had difficulties relating to the data and AI projects we described to them, they saw the technological development in the broader context of reforming the agency and their experiences with individual case workers over the years. The technology was not seen in isolation but representing a general approach to job seekers, namely standardised treatment with little adjustment to individual needs of the job seekers. The interviewees also recognised the structural transformation of the employment services as constrained to qualitative and individually adjusted support.

From Security Promises to Perceived Uncertainties: Example of Predictive Policing

Beyond the employment services, security and safety are of high concern for many citizens. While individuals may not have direct encounters with law enforcement on a daily basis, the topic of security holds significance for every citizen. Findings from the qualitative study emphasise that applying ADM in the law enforcement, predictive policing extends beyond identifying potential locations or individuals for future crimes and implementing preventive measures. It also has broader implications for overall police work and police–community relations (see also Masso et al., 2024).

In parallel with eliciting people's perspectives on potential future scenarios and their so-called agreements and opinions on future trends through a quantitative survey, we complemented our research with original qualitative enquiries. Much like the constructed scenarios in the quantitative study, we developed fictional narratives for this qualitative research. These stories were designed to mirror specific everyday situations, and we invited participants to complete these narratives based on their own experiences, attitudes and expectations. Similar to the approach in quantitative research, it is crucial to emphasise that these stories do not depict actual futures. Instead, they offer insights into people's expectations, concerns and their stance regarding the implementation of ADM solutions. We conducted a qualitative study among students as young experts who may potentially enter the public sector to develop or use automated decision-making systems, or among educated and critical citizens who could be potential users or target groups for these solutions (Masso et al., 2024).

A common thread in the citizens' narratives, elicited through prompts to complete stories involving everyday situations where predictive data technologies were employed, highlights the potential for police visits to generate stress, pressure and even paranoia among individuals, ultimately leading them to engage in criminal behaviour. Notably, one account from a study participant details a tragic outcome – a suicide following multiple visits by police officers who conveyed that analysis results were increasingly pointing towards the individual. Some narratives also highlight a performative aspect, where predictive policing, rather than accurately predicting crimes, influences individuals to engage in criminal activities. For instance, as described by a study participant in the story, Tom, the fictional target of police attention, reflects on the impact of police visits:

> The constant stress about him [Tom] committing a crime eventually got to him. He decided he needed it to happen already, just so that he could stop the constant anxiety. Later that night, he broke into a store and stood there waiting for the police to come to arrest him. After he was handcuffed, he finally felt relieved and stress-free. (public administration student from Estonia)

The narrative suggests that making assumptions about potential criminal activities resulted in a loss of trust in both the police and society. In some instances, a police visit was perceived as provocative rather than preventive in addressing future crimes. Quantitative survey data further unveil a significant association between trust in the police as an institution and support for the automation of police work. The findings indicate that increased trust in the police correlates with a higher level of agreement with the automation of policing ($p < 0.001$). Consequently, when citizens harbour scepticism towards the police as a state institution, the adoption of automation can exacerbate the distance between citizens and the state.

Another consequence of predictive policing, in addition to influencing trust in the police, is the potential for organisational changes within the police itself. Participants in the story completion study conveyed that predictive policing prioritises data over human judgement within the police force, potentially altering perceptions of police expertise. In one story, the fictional police officer Adam examines a list of potential criminals and observes discrepancies in some names. The narrative unfolds as follows:

> He (Adam) went back to the data analyst who shared those profiles and asked him how these lists started, and he (the data analyst) said 'It is above your paygrade, just do your thing, and that is it. The narrative underscores potential shifts in relationships within the police organization, where traditional police expertise is devalued, and a data analyst dictates tasks to a police officer. In this scenario, the police officer, Adam, actively seeks to understand the predictive system. However, the data analyst, presumed to hold a higher position in the predictive policing environment, dismisses Adam rudely without providing additional information. (media and communication student from Sweden)

This example highlights the diminishing role of human elements in decision-making processes as automated platforms take precedence. Despite Adam's intent as a police officer to comprehend the system for effective job execution, the data analyst, representing a more techno-focused perspective, denies him this opportunity and insists on following the indications of predictive analytics.

Some narratives redefined the objective of predictive policing, moving away from merely predicting crimes to identifying individuals who may require support to prevent them from engaging in criminal activities. In essence, these stories envisioned the police's role not solely focused on security but expanded to include elements of social services. For instance, in the next story, featuring Tom as a potential target, initial scepticism towards predictive policing evolves into a reflection on its potential benefit:

> If some of these people that end up in the statistics are depressed, sick – or in need of some help that they otherwise don't dare ask the authorities for – such as abuse, neglect, or discrimination, it makes the authorities more involved with society. Makes people feel heard and understood, therefore potentially preventing more crimes. (media and communication student from Sweden)

In this narrative, the acceptance and desirability of predictive policing are contingent upon the police assuming a role more aligned with social work than traditional security-related functions. This example highlights a significant outcome of predictive policing, blurring the delineation between security and social work within policing.

Such a shift in the conception of the police resonates with a Foucauldian perspective (Foucault, 1995), framing the police as a method for population management.

On the other hand, our findings also underscore widespread resistance to predictive policing technologies, with individuals expressing a desire for accountability and compensation in the event of failures. For instance, 92% of Estonian respondents from the quantitative survey advocated for compensation in case of potential inaccuracies, while the corresponding figure for Swedish respondents was 74%. This discrepancy may be attributed to Estonians' higher trust levels (Kerikmäe et al., 2019) and technological proficiency, making data-driven decision-making errors less forgivable.

While the story completion study did not reflect significant differences observed in survey data, it revealed similar resistance patterns among participants. Targets of predictive policing or even the police officers themselves engaged in activities expressing discontent, including imagining complaint letters, seeking help from data activists, suing the police department and resorting to conversations, or even physical altercations, with peers and officers. Some participants employed tactics such as VPN (virtual private network) usage, providing inaccurate information to the police, deleting internet histories and asserting their constitutional rights. In one story, the interviewee depicted Tom's efforts to avoid trouble and support his broken family, sharing a narrative that captured the challenges posed by predictive policing.

> Tom knew what he needed to do – he had read about some data scientists who were very vocal about something similar and as luck would have it they were organising a Q&A in a local community centre. If somebody knew how all of this worked and how to stop it, it would be them. (public administration student from Estonia)

As inferred from the narrative, the public administration student, representing here young experts potentially implementing the ADM solutions, endeavours to become more knowledgeable about predictive policing to explore ways to counteract it. Drawing parallels with similar strategies where individuals join forces with data activists, sue relevant authorities or compose complaint letters, it can be posited that participants sought to envision democratic avenues for halting predictive policing. This collective approach indicates a conscious recognition of the potential ramifications of technology and the potential for joint action against adverse effects.

Resistance against predictive policing was not limited to potential subjects alone. In certain stories, the assigned police officer, Adam, also expressed resistance, posing additional enquiries, seeking advice from colleagues and exhibiting a desire to understand the intricacies of predictive policing. In a narrative by SWE7, Adam raised concerns about privacy and potential biases in the data, prompting him to bring up the issue with his superiors. As one study participant from Sweden articulated:

His (Adam's) moral compass voted against personal monitoring, as that seemed even more invasive. He raised his concerns with those above him in rank and was met with sympathy. However, the decision was already made, and he had little to no say in it. It was up to him to execute the task in the most sensible way possible. (a media and communication student from Sweden)

This narrative underscores the potential influence that police officers may wield in the adoption of new technologies. While acknowledging the constraints on Adam's ability to alter the trajectory of events, specifically the implementation of predictive policing, the story notes his initial attempt to remove the technology and subsequent decision to execute his tasks judiciously. This can be interpreted as the participant's expectation from law enforcement officials or authorities employing such technologies. Even in situations where complete elimination proves challenging, there is an expectation that those in charge can apply these technologies more responsibly.

The analysis reveals a prevailing desire for open discussions surrounding the platformisation of police work and, in cases of failure, a call for review, change and potential elimination. Across many stories, individuals sought avenues to alter the application and usage of predictive policing. There was an expectation for the involvement of regular citizens, potential targets and police officers, the users of these technologies, in decision-making processes related to predictive policing. People anticipated accountability, desiring access to authorities and experts capable of addressing their queries, modifying certain practices and safeguarding the rights of citizens.

In summary, citizens studied in Estonia and Sweden demonstrate a certain willingness to implement ADM for crime prediction. However, participants in the study emphasised the need for additional human oversight due to the unpredictable outcomes of automation. Consequently, with the increased use of data analysis platforms in police work, noticeable shifts in trust towards the police as an institution and organisation are observed. Particularly, when citizens lack trust in the police as a state institution, the introduction of ADM may exacerbate the distance between the state and its citizens. A significant consequence of this 'abstract' perception of the police by citizens has been a sense of being under pressure and controlled. While some participants express acceptance of constant surveillance, others have developed various resistance patterns (see also Chapter 2).

Citizens actively resist the transformations underway in policing as data integration, analysis and visualisation platforms become more prevalent. Study participants, distinguished by their higher education levels and critical reflexivity skills, underscore the significance of actively collaborating with relevant authorities to shape predictive policing practices. This imperative for critical engagement extends not only to the targeted individuals but also to the police officers themselves. Various forms of resistance manifest, such as filing complaints, live-streaming interactions with officers, seeking guidance from higher-ranking officials and pursuing education from data experts. Additionally, there are endeavours to monitor or counter-monitor police actions.

This proactive approach, holding police departments accountable, is argued to foster more measured behaviour and professionalism among officers (Singh, 2017). The willingness to engage with predictive policing reflects a commitment to upholding accountability and transparency, emphasising democratic technological processes that safeguard citizens' rights rather than relying solely on technology to address societal issues.

Conclusions

In this chapter, we have engaged with mundane forms of negotiating and attempts at reforming the data welfare state from the perspective of journalists, unions and citizens being exposed to the data welfare state. Bringing the diverse perspectives together ranging from litigation cases to critical mapping initiatives and controversial interactions with and positioning against public agencies illustrates the broad span of how the data welfare state might be renegotiated and changes. The analysis also illustrate that there are creative and critical ways of how citizens and social actors are trying to shape the outlook of the data welfare state. As the first reforms for establishing welfare states, change is an active process that is based on practices and engagement by people affected. This might include forms of what we traditionally have considered as activism targeting specific reforms but also critical ways of relating to ADM in certain domains including predictive policing.

This chapter also makes a methodological point. As black boxed technologies such as AI and ADM are difficult to relate to for citizens, we decided to employ creative methods including future scenarios and story concluding methods to allow for in-depth engagement of our research participants. Illustrating potential consequences across domains through scenarios and vignettes opened a space of conversation. Particularly helpful were also the story concluding sessions for which we triangulated the qualitative material with findings from our survey material for further contextualisation.

References

Akademikerförbundet SSR. (2020). Tillsätt en algoritmombudsman. https://akademssr.se/post/tillsatt-en-algoritmombudsman

Akademikerförbundet SSR. (2024). Din kollega har blivit en algoritm. Digitalisering, AI och automatisering från ett fackligt perspektiv. https://akademssr.se/sites/default/files/files/Din%20kollega%20har%20blivit%20en%20algoritm_andra%20upplagan.pdf

AlgorithmWatch. (2019). *Automating Society 2019*. Report. https://algorithmwatch.org/en/automating-society-2019/

AlgorithmWatch. (2020). *Automating Society 2020*. Report. https://automatingsociety.algorithmwatch.org/wp-content/uploads/2020/12/Automating-Society-Report-2020.pdf

Alston, P. (2019) *report of the special rapporteur on extreme poverty and human rights*. https://www.ohchr.org/EN/newyork/_layouts/15/WopiFrame.aspx?sourcedoc=/EN/newyork/Documents/GA74/A_74_48037.docx&action=default&DefaultItemOpen=1

Bonini, T., & Treré, E. (2024). *Algorithms of resistance: The everyday fight against platform power*. Mit Press.

Carlsson, V. (2023). Legal certainty in automated decision-making in welfare services. *Public Policy and Administration*. https://doi.org/10.1177/09520767231202334.

Couldry, N. (2024). Data as narrative: Contesting the right to the word, *Social Movement Studies*. https://doi.org/10.1080/14742837.2024.2328581

Dagenssamhälle. (2020). *Känsliga uppgifter spreds via kod till biståndsrobot* [Sensitive data were distributed via code of a benefit robot]. https://www.dagenssamhalle.se/nyhet/kansliga-uppgifter-spreds-kod-till-bistandsrobot-31911?fbclid=IwAR3LsYY0uxmI64JR9yDSh4sFgSlwj6HvCq2UY7ABPbPCWU3rqpjcLsrdfAk

Dubois, V. (2016). *The bureaucrat and the poor: Encounters in French welfare offices*. Routledge.

European Commission, Joint Research Centre (JRC) (2021): *Selected AI cases in the public sector*. European Commission, Joint Research Centre (JRC). http://data.europa.eu/89h/7342ea15-fd4f-4184-9603-98bd87d8239a

Foucault, M. (1995). *Discipline & punish: The birth of the prison* (A. Sheridan, Trans.). Vintage Books.

Hepp, A., & Görland, S. O. (2024). Agency in a datafied society: An introduction. *Convergence*. https://doi.org/10.1177/13548565241254692

Jarvis, M. D. (2014). The black box of bureaucracy: Interrogating accountability in the public service. *Australian Journal of Public Administration*, *73*, 450–466. https://doi.org/10.1111/1467-8500.12109

Kaun, A. (2022). Suing the algorithm: The mundanization of automated decision-making in public services through litigation, information, *Communications Society*, *25*(14), 2046–2062, https://doi.org/10.1080/1369118X.2021.1924827

Kaun, A., Männiste, M., & Liminga, A. (2023). *Mapping the automated decision-making landscape in Swedish and Estonian welfare state*. Available at: http://sh.diva-portal.org/smash/get/diva2:1789852/FULLTEXT02.pdf

Kerikmäe, T., Troitiño, D., & Shumilo, O. (2019). An Idol or an ideal? A case study of Estonian E-governance: Public perceptions, myths and misbeliefs. *Acta Baltica Historiae et Philosophiae Scientiarum*, *7*(1), 71–80.

Masso, A., Kasapoglu, T., Kaun, A., & Galis, V. (2024). Citizens' perspectives on platformisation of police work: A scenario and story-based exploration in Estonia and Sweden. *Article Draft under Review in Journal Information, Communication and Society*. https://doi.org/10.1177/14407833241234675

Männiste, M., & Masso, A. (2020). 'Three drops of blood for the devil': Data pioneers as intermediaries of algorithmic governance ideals. *Mediální Studia (Media Studies)*, *14*(1), 55–74.

Redden, J. (2018). Democratic governance in an age of datafication: Lessons from mapping government discourses and practices. *Big Data & Society*, *5*(2). https://doi.org/10.1177/2053951718809145

Redden, J., Brand, J., Sander, I., Warne, H., Grant, A., & White, D. (2022). Automating public services: Learning from cancelled systems. Data Justice Lab, Cardiff University.

Singh, A. (2017). Prolepticon: Anticipatory citizen surveillance of the police. *Surveillance and Society, 15*(5), 676–688. https://doi.org/10.24908/ss.v15i5.6418

SOU (2018). Juridik som stöd för förvaltningens digitalisering. https://www.regeringen.se/contentassets/e9a0044c745c4c9ca84fef309feafd76/juridik-som-stod-for-forvaltningens-digitalisering-sou-201825.pdf

Svensson, L. (2019). *'Tekniken är den enkla biten': Om att implementera digital automatisering i handläggningen av försörjningsstöd*. Socialhögskolan, Lunds universitet.

Tammpuu, P., & Masso, A. (2018). 'Welcome to the virtual state': Estonian e-residency and the digitalised state as a commodity. *European Journal of Cultural Studies, 21*(5), 543–560. https://doi.org/10.1177/1367549417751148

Trifuljesko, S. (2022). Things of AI Ethics: Algorithm and AI Register in Amsterdam and Helsinki. In *Presentation ADM Institutionalised: Public Sector Governance*. 6–7 April 2022, Lund University.

Conclusion: Crisis in the Welfare Question: Rethinking the Welfare State in the Age of Automation

The title of this last chapter *'Crisis in the Question of Welfare'* makes references to some famous predecessors and pamphlets that addressed pressing societal issues such as Alva and Gunnar Myrdal's 1934 Crisis in the Population Question (Kris i befolkningsfrågan) as well as Ivar Lo-Johansson's 1949 Age – A Pamphlet (Ålderdom – En stridskrift). These works in many ways prepared and accompanied large-scale welfare reforms of the people's home in Sweden including day-care facilities for children and the reform of elderly care. They were part of a struggle to build the Swedish welfare state that did not just emerge out of nowhere but needed to be actively fought for. Similarly, we would like to end the book in a programmatic manner outlining an agenda for an engaged scholarship that contributes to a data welfare state serving the public good and that allows for a good life for all according to their needs and capabilities. This chapter has an explicit normative grounding in the needs and rights of people for human flourishing.

Throughout the book, we have engaged with experiences of and with the data welfare state, experiences by case workers, beneficiaries, citizens, and also those developing tools for datafication and automated decision-making (ADM). By drawing an overview of historical developments (Chapter 1) and engaging with use cases and implementation projects (Chapter 2) as well as experiences of citizens (Chapter 3) and forms of re-negotiating the data welfare state (Chapter 4), we highlight the emerging centrality of data for welfare provision across three different countries. Based on these enquiries, we suggest the notion of the data welfare state that aims to capture important shifts in how welfare is organised and delivered to the citizens. We redefine welfare as entangled with data practices that mediated ideas about what welfare is and how it should be achieved. Data-based, digital infrastructures are hence not merely administrative tools, but part of a large-scale shift in welfare organisation. Chapter 1 delved into structural aspects of the data welfare state and its historical roots as well as national variations. The second chapter zoomed in on implementation projects in Sweden and Estonia to trace the ambivalent process of mundanisation, for example, turning new technologies into everyday tools. The third chapter in contrast took citizen perspectives as a starting point to carve out different positions about and within the welfare state that reflect national differences as well as social positions. The fourth chapter engaged with active attempts to reshape and form the data welfare state according to the specific needs of citizens. It dived into forms of renegotiation and resistance against the data welfare state.

Based on these empirical enquiries and conceptual work, we propose the following definition for the data welfare state. **The data welfare state and the automation of welfare refer to a fundamental social change towards using data-based technologies to shape people's daily well-being and enhance their quality of life, while considering the potential vulnerability of all parties involved concerning data, digital technologies and automation.** The definition broadens the understanding of welfare beyond social rights emphasising an expansive understanding of welfare. With this broad definition and approach, we aim to underline three key aspects, which are crucial in any work within the public sector and beyond, focusing on welfare and data: (1) enhancing well-being and improving quality of life, (2) involving multiple parties in the welfare provision project and (3) the potential for vulnerability (emphasising not only the concept of vulnerability but also the term 'potential'). We will explain these emphases in more detail, based on the empirical research results analysed and presented in this book (see also Table 5.1).

First, we would like to underline the fundamental process of change that accompanies welfare automation projects. As discussed in this book, the introduction of welfare automation should be viewed against the broader backdrop of historical and societal processes that have either made these solutions possible or created unfavourable conditions for their implementation (see Chapter 1). This is not merely a matter of changes in organisational practices or the adoption of new data infrastructure solutions but rather involves fundamental social and cultural shifts that either enable these changes or push the welfare state into crisis or a new threshold (see Chapter 4 or the summary introduction). A notable example includes potential value or trust conflicts (see Chapter 2), friction (Chapter 2), negotiations and resistances (Chapter 4), which we have analysed in this book.

Secondly, we wish to emphasise the importance of involving multiple parties in the welfare provision project. This means considering the awareness, perspectives, skills, practices, trust, norms and values of both those who develop ADM solutions and those who are the target group or users of these computational solutions. The significance of involving these multiple stakeholders is highlighted by the concept of triple agency used in the book (Masso & Kasapoglu, 2020, see also Chapter 1), which illustrates that it is essential to address not only the potential vulnerability of data subjects who are the targets of the ADM solutions, but also the vulnerability of experts, such as case workers, who are developing these tools. These experts are often under pressure to make correct and fair decisions while mediating computational system solutions to the end target group. For example, based on the empirical enquiries analysed and presented in this book, we have observed shifts in the work of civil servants, case workers and employees in the public sector more generally, but we have also seen creative and critical ways of relating to data welfare infrastructures negotiating and partly resisting them to improve their outcomes.

Another important outcome of our empirical work is the importance of highlighting the relationality of the elements that constitute the data welfare state. Not only are all data interconnected, even though they are produced by separate entities within the state, but they are also networked and come at certain costs. Additionally, the social interaction processes, involving multiple stakeholders such as developers and decision-makers who develop and plan these solutions, as well as potential users or target groups of these solutions, are crucial. Without the close cooperation of these stakeholders and ongoing negotiations about norms, values and practices, it is challenging to create welfare that considers the needs, principles, readiness and values of different groups. We must also take into account the interplay between various social processes that influence data welfare, whether these involve technological changes such as the development of new machine learning models, institutional changes like the shift towards data-driven organizational cultures, or cultural shifts in people's trust towards public institutions in relation to the implementation of ADM.

And thirdly, we wish to emphasise the potential vulnerability that may accompany any data welfare and automation project. At the same time, vulnerability is a contested notion and is often used in prescriptive ways pointing out, for example, 'especially vulnerable groups' in ethic reviews. We stress that this is not a prescriptive or normative category, but rather a layered and relational phenomenon. The nature of precarity does not necessarily manifest universally but is expressed in specific social, temporal and spatial contexts, domains and situations. Martha Fineman stresses that vulnerability is a human condition to refocus the discussions. Instead of using vulnerability in stigmatising or prescriptive ways, she argues that 'vulnerability is universal, constant, and inherent to the human condition' (Fineman, 2010). Further, she argues that while vulnerability is universal, it is experienced in particular and very individual ways as 'we have different forms of embodiment and are differently situated within webs of economic and institutional relationships'. How vulnerabilities are experienced varies between individuals and their experiences are unique. However, understanding vulnerability itself as a universal human condition asks for new solidarities across different social groups and shifts the focus towards the institutional structures that uphold or produce vulnerabilities or can counter them rather than remaining on the individual level. As Fineman argues, vulnerability '(...) moves us beyond identity-based inquiries because it focuses not only on discrimination against defined groups but is also concerned with the privileges conferred on limited segments of the population by the state through its institutions'. In contrast, Levine et al. (2004) dismiss the notion of vulnerability as limited labelling that has lost all practical meaning. There are now so many 'official' vulnerable groups that basically everyone is somehow a vulnerable subject, they argue. This makes any meaningful use of vulnerability impossible. This argument is countered by Florencia Luna (2019), who argues for a definition of vulnerability based on layers and cascades of vulnerability that provide further nuance to the discussion rather than dismissing vulnerability completely. However, Luna remains critical of a too fine-grained and too functional definition of vulnerability. She goes into an argument with Lange et al., 2013 who propose a taxonomy of vulnerability, and she argues that this is not meaningful and cannot capture the full complexity of human life. Instead, we should rather stay with layers and cascades of vulnerability.

Therefore, besides this particularistic approach to vulnerabilities proposed by Levine, and universal approach introduced by Fineman, the third approach of Luna emphasises that vulnerabilities is a layered phenomenon (please see Wetzig, 2024 for an overview).

Here, we follow Martha Fineman's approach, which helps refocus welfare automation projects from data infrastructure and state efficiency to the potential human and social conditions that are at the core of any welfare automation project. Additionally, we draw on Luna's layered approach to vulnerability, which emphasises the contextual and relational aspects that proved crucial in our comparative analysis (see, e.g. Chapter 3). Florencia Luna critiques the particularistic approach for creating too many categories and the universal approach for rendering everyone unprotectable. Instead, Luna proposes a dynamic, contextual and relational understanding of vulnerability. She argues that vulnerability is not fixed or general but varies based on individual circumstances. Luna's approach involves identifying and evaluating layers of vulnerability to develop strategies addressing them. Her approach integrates other definitions of vulnerability, focusing on dispositions to harm that can be actualised or remain dormant, triggered by specific conditions. Luna also emphasises that responses should prioritise and address layers of vulnerability, aiming to avoid exacerbation and ideally minimise or eradicate them.

Nevertheless, we emphasise the term 'potential' – vulnerability is neither universal nor particularistic, meaning it is not inherently tied to specific social categories but can manifest in certain situations.

As we have demonstrated throughout the book, datafication and digital technologies introduce new layers of vulnerability (see also Wetzig, 2024). These data vulnerabilities need to be acknowledged and identified to be managed and mitigated or resisted against. Acknowledging that we are all vulnerable and sharing data vulnerabilities means to foreground a call for a broad solidarity across contexts. This broad solidarity is essential if we want to build just and equal societies. However, with our data welfare state definition, we aim to show that welfare automation and the data welfare state are neither inherently 'bad' nor 'good', but represent an ongoing and dynamic process of social change. A critical assessment of the underlying infrastructural and social processes, allows for not only the prevention and response to negative outcomes but also a focus on the creation of welfare itself.

Additionally, the comparative outlook of our study has highlighted that context matters for both how ADM and algorithmic automation are introduced by also how it is experienced by the people. Data-based technologies constitute intersection and

Table 5.1 Three Data Welfare State Systems and Social Vulnerabilities

	Estonia	Germany	Sweden
Enhancing well-being and improving quality of life	A not yet crystallised, rather liberal understanding of welfare	Stratified understanding and practices to welfare, well-being	Well-being and equality as universal ideals in the society
Multiple stakeholders in the welfare provision projects	Data pioneers, activists in the PA institutions, citizens	Citizens, corporate groups, human rights organisations	Citizens, trade unions, human rights organisations
Potential vulnerabilities	Vulnerabilities depending on the domain, where ADM is implemented, particularistic understanding of vulnerabilities.	Citizens in general who are cautious in regard of ADM, perceived universal vulnerabilities	Vulnerabilities of certain social categories (e.g. immigrants, unemployed people), the layered and intersectional understanding of vulnerabilities.

Source: Authors' table.
Note: ADM, automated decision-making; PA, public administration.

multilevel mediations for which the country context, the domain context and the context of people's lifeworld matter. Therefore, the manifestations of the welfare state depend largely on the social context, considering structural, social and cultural conditions, as we can see from Table 5.1. Therefore, different understandings of vulnerabilities, meanings of welfare, and the role of stakeholders in welfare provision projects can vary significantly.

With a focus on the frictions that emerge in the datafication process, as we analysed and illustrated using the three data welfare state systems, we have seen that many of the experiences that we encountered highlight shared vulnerabilities, namely vulnerabilities that relate to data and automation infrastructures, and vulnerabilities that relate to potential harms and threats in and through digital infrastructures. By closing the book, we zoom in on the notion of data vulnerability within the data welfare state and propose concrete practical suggestions for the future of the data welfare state.

Three Propositions for the Data Welfare State

To meet the emerging data vulnerabilities, we make three propositions:

1) Without real welfare no data welfare
2) Without a focus on people no data welfare
3) Without public data infrastructures no data welfare

1# The first proposition is related to the argument that the development of datafication and digitalisation and the welfare state are entangled. The societies that have been in focus here have experienced the dismantling of their welfare systems since the late 1970s with the emergence of neoliberal politics. Data welfare is emerging in the context of austerity and shrinking investments in shared resources for welfare provision. This is reflected in a stronger focus on control rather than care that data infrastructures enable. In Sweden, for example, the idea of universal access to welfare is replaced with a discourse on welfare fraud and control of welfare beneficiaries. Just recently, a new public agency was formed after the Danish model to identify welfare fraud relying primarily on data analytics. Different actors quote sources estimating the costs for welfare fraud between 14 and 28 billion Swedish Krona per year, which constituted two to four percent of all benefit payments within the welfare system. How the figures are calculated remains unclear. If the data welfare state is supposed to be just and promote the capabilities for all, the starting point cannot be fraudulent practices. Instead, the data welfare state needs to focus on the specific needs of the people.

#2 If the needs and capabilities are in focus, the data welfare state must be grounded in the lived experiences of the people. Rather than finding problems to technological solutions that are decoupled from the people, we need to turn the datafication process on its head and start from the peoples' perspective. What is meaningful and necessary in their lives? How can data and digital infrastructures be supportive? But also, how can they be designed in ways that are intuitive and accessible for the people? This re-centring of people in the automation and datafication process implies a shift in the methods and forms of implementation, where citizens must play a larger role. Focusing on individuals involves considering both the target audience for potential automated solutions and supporting active data activists who voluntarily contribute their data for informed decision-making in the public sector, as seen in reflexive data disclosure. This also entails raising citizens' awareness about data collected about them for ADM purposes. Focusing on individuals involves not only accommodating the preferences of the target audience for data solutions but also acknowledging the potential vulnerability of data experts and decision-makers who, as illustrated vividly by the analysis of the Estonian case, must make accurate and equitable decisions in uncertain situations when utilising data solutions.

#3 The data welfare state needs to be built on public infrastructures that are owned, maintained and developed by public actors. The starting points for the technologies that are used within the welfare systems cannot be based on profit-maximising principles but need to follow public values. Consequently, the overly strong reliance on big tech players, in the Swedish public sector, for example, primarily Microsoft, needs to be critically reconsidered. All components from the data centres, the cable infrastructures to cloud solutions, need to run on the terms of the public values rather than commercial interests since opting out – that is sometimes proposed for social media platforms or other digital infrastructures that are coming for our data – is not an option in the context of the welfare state. In addition to the envisioned ideal of creating public data infrastructures within the European data spaces (European Union, 2024), which establishes not only norms, principles and examples of best practices in data sharing, it is crucial to create favourable conditions for the establishment of data cooperatives based on individual initiatives and the sharing of data as commons.

CONCLUSION

We close the book with an extract of a poem written by Göran Greider – a Swedish author, journalist and political commentator. In 1995, Greider was hoping to see a better future for the Swedish people's home. Arguing that the long period of dismantling of welfare infrastructures and the rise of neoliberalism since the 1970s was only an interlude, he opened for a better future that has roots in the past. Similarly, we have shown that engagement matters for the re-shaping of our welfare infrastructures. Let us remain critically hopeful for the future.

A People's Home, a poem by Göran Greider, 1995[1]

(...)

The period from 1975 until today was a parenthesis.

It didn't give birth to any dreams larger than one's own life.

Now the new times are taking over, still unborn,

Partly because the picture of the past is still so strong:

The legacy of the people's home must be a goodbye, from the world, from the factories

(...)

Reality changes, not the deepest values.

For these values, indispensable, are alive

In that, we need to leave to make space for the new.

The breakup with this time 1945–75:

The final possibility of the past

References

Fineman, M. A. (2010). The vulnerable subject: Anchoring equality in the human condition. In *Transcending the boundaries of law* (pp. 177–191). Routledge-Cavendish.

European Union. (2024). *Common European Data Spaces | Building the single market for data.* https://digital-strategy.ec.europa.eu/en/policies/data-spaces

Greider, G. (1995). *När fabrikerna tystnar*. Albert Bonnier Förlag.

Lange, M. M., Rogers, W., & Dodds, S. (2013). Vulnerability in research ethics: A way forward. *Bioethics, 27*(6), 333–340.

---

[1]Translated by the authors.

Levine, C., Faden, R., Grady, C., Hammerschmidt, D., Eckenwiler, L., & Sugarman, J. (2004). The limitations of 'vulnerability' as a protection for human research participants. *The American Journal of Bioethics, 4*(3), 44–49.

Lo-Johansson, I. (1949). *Ålderdom – stridskrift* (Age – a pamphlet).

Luna, F. (2019). Identifying and evaluating layers of vulnerability–a way forward. *Developing World Bioethics, 19*(2), 86–95.

Masso, A., & Kasapoglu, T. (2020). Understanding power positions in a new digital landscape: Perceptions of Syrian refugees and data experts on relocation algorithm. *Information, Communication & Society, 23*(8), 1203–1219. https://doi.org/10.1080/1369118X.2020.1739731

Myrdal, G., & Myrdal, A. (1934). *Kris i befolkningsfrågan (Crisis in the population question).*

Wetzig, L. (2024). *From principle to practice: Understanding citizen-centricity in public service digitalisation through vulnerability. The case of German unemployment welfare services.* Master's thesis. Technology Governance & Sustainability, Tallinn University of Technology, https://digikogu.taltech.ee/et/item/0b74fa6a-e14a-4c07-844b-db9313a51fb4

Index

A
'Abstract' perception, 101
Abstractisation of state, 30 (table)
Accountability, 60
Accuracy, 50
Activism, 30
Activity reports, 53
Actual automation process, 48
Administrative Court, 91
Agar, J., 5
Agency, 19, 20 (figure)
'Agreeing conformists', 70, 73
'Algorithmic appreciation', 67
Algorithmic approach, 29
Algorithmic automated decision-making, 6
Algorithmic automation, 27
'Algorithmic culture', vii
Algorithmic decision-making, 91
Algorithmic governance, 6, 30, 60, 92
Algorithmic injustice, 27
Algorithmic public services
  automating benefit applications, 45–49
  automating Swedish public employment services, 49–56
  email signature image, 48 (figure)
  from magical creature 'Kratt' to personalised state, 56–61
  mundanisation, 9, 44–45
  from rebel to model, 45–49
Algorithmic systems, vii, 46, 59, 68
AlgorithmWatch, 90
Alison, W., 3
Allardt, E., 4
Andreassen, R., 7
Archer, M., 18
Arcy, J., 56
Artificial intelligence (AI), viii, 3, 23, 43, 65, 89, 97
Artificial intelligence values, 74
  descriptive statistics of, 75 (table)
  explanation of, 77 (table)
Assessment tool, 50
Automated decision-making (ADM), ix, 5–10, 29, 32, 44, 47, 50, 52, 65, 69, 72, 88, 92, 105
  risk perception, 72–73, 73 (figure)
  trust in, 70–72, 71 (figure)
Automated systems, 65

Automated tools, 58
Automated welfare state, 26, 34
Automating public services, 9
Automation, 3–4, 27
  automation-driven inequality, 27
  evolution of, 28
  process, 48, 68, 110
  projects, vii
  technologies, 16
Autonomy, 75–76
Awareness, 66, 69 (figure), 69–70

B
Bastani, A., 3
Benanva, A., 3
Big data, viii
Black box method, 60
Black box problem, 88
Bonini, T., 88
Bottom-up initiatives, 90

C
Care, 54–55, 57
  forms of, 46
  practices, 46
Carlsson, V., 51
Caseworkers, 51–52
ChatGPT, 68
Citizens care, 68–69
  awareness and suitability, 69–70
  about data welfare state, 67–68
  trust in automated decision-making, 70–73, 71 (figure)
  values, 73–78
Citizens' attitudes towards automation, typology based on, 78–79
Communication services, 3
Communicative AI, 65
Computation, 31
Computational models, 21
Computerisation, 7, 46
Context, 32, 66
  of automation, 16
  of data welfare, 16
  of implementing ADM, 76
  of welfare state, 27
Conversely, 76
Corporatist-statist welfare sate model, 8

Couldry, N., 88
Crisis, 7, 105
Critical data studies, 87
Critical engagement, 101
Criticisms, 46
'Cultural changes', 19
Cultural interactions, 19
Cultural practices, vii

D

Danish model, 110
Data, 21, 28
  acculturation, 18
  activism, 30
  collection, 8
  cooperatives, 110
  culture shift, 21
  data-based approach, 26
  data-based automation, 3, 43, 51
  data-based decision-making, 18, 27, 30–31
  data-based projects, 97
  data-based public administration, 43
  data-based solutions, 21
  data-based technologies, 6, 109
  data-based tools, 68
  data-driven decision-making, 30–31
  data-driven governance, 27
  data-informed approach, 26
  data-informed decision-making, 27, 30–31
  delegation, 45
  experts, 23
  infrastructure, 21
  justice lab, 89
  misuse, 27
  models, 19
  pioneers, 21
  sharing, 28
  skills, 2
  sources, 26
  space, 110
  studies, 19
  tools, 2, 44
  vulnerabilities, 108–109
Data welfare, 2, vii, 29
  advocates of efficiency, 79
  citizens care, 68–79
  experiences of, 9, 65
  informed avant-gardists, 80–81
  machine, 2
  risk-inexperienced skeptics, 79
  sample structure of survey, 66 (table)
  social sceptics, 80
  welfare watchdogs/vigilant welfare defenders, 80
Data welfare state, 6–7, 9–10, 16, 29, 44, 56, 88, 105

citizens care about, 67–68
comparison of, 30 (table), 33 (table)
controversial interactions with public agencies, 98–97
emergence of, 24, 31
evolution of, 23–29
examples of, 31
exploring data welfare state through future scenarios, 92–96, 93 (figure)
investigating and questioning data welfare state through litigation, 90–92
mapping and counter-mapping as methods, 89–90
systems, 109 (table)
three propositions for, 109–111
unravelling forces behind, 29–32
variations of, 32–34
Datafication, vii, 3–4, 6–7, 27, 88, 105, 108
  in driving social change, 17–23
  process, 109–110
Datafied welfare state, 5–10
Dataism, 4
Decentering technology, vii
Decision support systems, 6, 46, 58
Decision tree model, 46
Decision-making process, 31, 99
'Delayed' transformations, 21
Digital care, 55–56, 59
  work in Estonia, 57
Digital coaches, 54–55
Digital computing technologies, 17
Digital data, 28
Digital frictions, 2
'Digital housewife', 55
Digital infrastructures, 7
Digital platforms, 65
Digital social transformations, 18
Digital systems, 6
Digital tasks, 55
Digital technologies, 6, 9, 55
Digital transformation, 27–28
Digital welfare, ix, 2
Digitalisation, vii, 7, 31, 45–46, 90
Disruption, 17, 22
Diversity, 76

E

Economic transformation, 27
Education, 7, 94
Efficiency, 76–77, 79
Electronic services, 26
Elyachar, J., 56
Emerging projects, 6
Employment services, 52–55, 92
Equality, 18
Erkers, H., 92
Esping-Andersen, G., 4–5, 7

INDEX

Estonia, case of, 56–61
Estonian photographic heritage (FOTIS), 58
Estonians favour predictive policing, 95
Evidence-based decision-making, 27
Explainability, 75–76

F
Familiar dynamics, 27
Family-oriented individuals, 79
Fineman, M., 107
Forsman, M., 55
Frey, C. B., 3
Frictionless interaction, 2
Frictions, 2, 51–52, 58
Future scenarios, 92–96

G
Galis, V., ix
Gender, 95
General Data Protection Regulation (GDPR), 67
General digitalisation policies, 45
Görland, S. O., 88
Governance, ix, 19, 26–27
Governance renewal journey, 56
Greider, G., 111

H
Health, 5–7, 47, 58
Hepp, A., 88
Housing allowances, 4
Human-Centered Artificial Intelligence Centre, 90
'Human-centred government', 60

I
Individual citizens, 91
'Individuals' lifeworlds, 33 (table)
Industrial revolution, 3
Informed avant-gardists, 80–81
'Informed sceptics', 70, 72–73
Innovation, ix, 21, 47
Inspektionen för arbetslöshetsförsäkringen (IAF), 52
Institutionalisation, 30
Internal practices, 53
Interoperability, 76
Intertwined historical process, 26
Interviews, 23, 47–48, 51, 96–97

J
Jarrett, K., 55
Job seeker, 51, 96
Joint Research Centre (JRC), 90
Justice, 18
Justification, 89

K
Kalm, S., 55
Kasapoglu, T., ix
Kaun, A., ix, 55
Kratt, 57–58
   care, 57–58
   failures, 58–61
   frictions, 58

L
Larsson, A. O., ix
Layered vulnerability, 108
Levine, C., 107
Liminga, A., ix
Lindert, P. H., 4–5
Litigation, questioning data welfare state through, 90–92
   litigation, 90–92
Long-term unemployed, experiences of, 96–97
Luna, F., 108

M
Machine learning
   algorithms, 60
   models, 32
   techniques, 21
Mainstream media, 47
Malinowski, B., 56
Männiste, M., ix
Marshall's, T. H., 4
Masso, A., ix
Meaning-making around technology, 44
Medical experts, 23
Microsoft, 110
Modern social policy, 24
Mundanisation process, 9, 44–45, 106
   automating benefit applications, 45–49
   automating Swedish public employment services, 49–56

O
Open data
   government, 28
   platforms, 28
   sharing, 28
Organisational transformation, 49
Organizational data culture, 18
OTT, 58–59

P
Parliamentary Ombudsman (PO), 91
Particularistic approach, 108
Personal interests, protection of, 76
Platformisation, 27, 101
Polanyi, K., 5
Police work, 9

Political transformation, 27
Positive coefficients, 94
Post-communist welfare regimes, viii
Predictive policing, 96
  example of, 97–102
  scenario, 92
Public administration, 27, 68, 91, 100
Public agencies, 2, 96–97
Public Employment Services in Sweden, 49
Public sector automation, historical foundations of, 25 (figure)
Public service automation in driving social change, 17–23
Public services, 30
Puig de la Bellacasa, M., 55

Q
Quantitative research, 94
Quantitative survey data, 98, 100

R
(Re-)configuring data welfare, 10
  controversial interactions with public agencies, 96–97
  exploring data welfare state through future scenarios, 92–96
  investigating and questioning data welfare state through litigation, 90–92
  mapping and counter-mapping as methods to critically engage with data welfare state, 89–90
  from security promises to perceived uncertainties, 97–102
Redden, J., 89
Research methods, 67, 98
Risks, 23, 70, 89
  perception, 66, 72–73, 73 (figure)
  risk-inexperienced skeptics, 79
Robotic process automation (RPA), 9, 43, 50
Ruckenstein, M., 2

S
Scenarios, 92–96
Security, 97–102
Singh, R., 56
Smart technology, viii
'Smart' digitalization, 6
Smartification of state, 88
Social changes, 16–17, 22
Social context, 32
Social datafication, 16
Social diversity, 77
Social insurance, 5
Social Insurance Agency, 53
Social interactions, 19

Social media, 56
Social movements, 88
Social policies, 5
Social sceptics, 80
Social transformations, viii, 16–19, 21
Social welfare, 3, 26
Social-democratic welfare state model, 7–8
Societal transformation, 27
Socio-demographic variables, 78
Sociotechnical imaginaries, 44
Software development, vii
Solidarity, 76
State-citizen relations, 10, 22
State-individual relationship, 29
Structural changes, 19, 45
Structure, agency and culture (SAC), 19
Suitability, 69 (figure), 69–70
Survey data, 66
Sustainability, 18, 75–77
Svensson, L., 90
Sweden's social democratic welfare regime, 95
Swedish public employment services
  automating, 49–50
  care, 54–56
  failure, 52–54
  frictions, 51–52
  variables that calculate job chances of registered job seekers, 50 (figure)
Swedish welfare state, 105

T
Tallinn University of Technology (TalTech), ix
Technically precise terminology, 48
Technologies, 44–45, 97
Theoretical–methodological framework, 19
'Tiger Leap', 57
Top-down initiatives, 89
'Train and match'
  employment tool, 51
  programme, 50
Transparency, 60
Trelleborg model, 45, 90
Trelleborg municipality, 45–46, 48, 91
Treré, E., 88
Trifuljesko, S., 89
Triple agency, 19, 106
Tronto, J. C., 55
Trust
  in automated decision-making (ADM), 70–73, 71 (figure)
  in institutions, 79
Typology based on citizens' attitudes towards automation, 78–79

INDEX

U
Unemployment insurance payment, 53
Universal solidarity, 76

V
Values, 73–78
　conflicts, 32
　embeddedness, 74
van Noordt, C., ix
Vigilant welfare defenders, 80
Vinge, S., 92
Virtual private network (VPN), 100
Vulnerability, 107–108

W
Wajcman, J., 3
Welfare, 4–5, 75–76, 105
　data-based automation and, 3
　datafication, 23
　domains, 5–6
　infrastructures, 111
　systems, 23
　watchdogs, 80
Welfare automation, 16–17, 23
　data tools for, 44
　initiatives, vii
　projects, 16
　transformative mechanisms of, 20 (figure)
　variations of, 32–34
Welfare state, 5, 26–27
　automation, 16
　comparison of, 30 (table)
　ideals, 26
　model, 23
　transformation, ix
Williams, R., 4
Willim, R., 43–44

X
'X-road', 57